Incarnation
&
Metamorphosis

Incarnation
&
Metamorphosis

Can Literature Change Us?

DAVID MASON

PAUL DRY BOOKS
Philadelphia 2023

First Paul Dry Books Edition, 2023

Paul Dry Books, Inc.
Philadelphia, Pennsylvania
www.pauldrybooks.com

ISBN: 978-1-58988-172-3

Library of Congress Control Number: 2022949018

Printed in the United States of America

For Chrissy

Contents

PART TWO

Voices, Dead and Living

Incarnation
&
Metamorphosis

Introduction

What do we know but that we face
One another in this place?

   —W. B. YEATS

THIS IS A BOOK about living with literature, both reading and writing, paying attention to the world without immediately rushing to judge it. It's about hearing voices, singly and in chorus, telling stories that make connections between literature and life. Literature is a kind of embodiment, and embodiment means change. But what we mean by change is not always easy to say or to hear, so we must be patient as we look at the examples of others. Some of these essays examine life and literature in broad terms, and others are about the lives of specific writers whose successes and failures have much to teach us. Above all, I want to suggest that the values of literature—verbal precision, beauty, and the courage to face life in all its variety and ambiguity—are worth holding, and are perhaps even civilizing in the rigor and compassion they demand of us.

Consider the example of one great, often-unfashionable writer. In the months leading up to his death on January 28,

1939, William Butler Yeats wrote some of the best poems of his life. He presents a wonderful example of literary vigor into old age, though in our time we wouldn't necessarily call him old—he died at 73, his heart exhausted from a strenuous life. Among the last poems were several probing the place of poetry in both public and private spheres, the relationship of art and politics. He asked in "Man and the Echo," "Did that play of mine send out / Certain men the English shot?" Yeats knew very well that when patriots like Padraig Pearse and Thomas MacDonagh staged their failed rebellion in Easter Week, 1916, they were, as literary men, inspired by the literature and art of the Celtic Renaissance. But he could not know whether his words literally produced their revolutionary fervor.

Can a work of literature effect social and political change? The play Yeats mentions, *Cathleen ni Houlihan*, can be read as Irish republican propaganda only by readers blind to ambiguity. We can also see the "Mother Ireland" figure in the play as a monster devouring young men, leading them needlessly to slaughter in a cult of political violence. Yeats might have been a skeptic about the political efficacy of literature, but not about its importance to society, the ways we see ourselves reflected in the arts. Did his play, he wondered, inspire a revolt? The question keeps him awake at night in the mind's echo chamber, where sounds take on multiple meanings—a condition of both great art and old age.

Put another way, can literature change *us*? In his elegy for Yeats, W. H. Auden said that on the one hand "Poetry makes nothing happen," and on the other it is "a way of happening." But Auden was writing poetry, and Yeats's question concerns a play: a different kind of art, in which a community of people sitting together is presented with dramatic reflections of life. An old friend of mine, a Dubliner named John Devitt, often opined that the Abbey Theatre had done as much to create modern Ireland as all the guns and bombs of the nationalists. Maybe so. Communal arts like theater might well have a different kind of power, especially in an era not suffering a pandemic, when people are allowed to sit shoulder to shoulder, sharing the catharsis with live bodies moving and speaking on stage. Yet the question remains a nagging one for all of us. In my own reading life, I have often felt most captivated by literature in which something more than the personal is at stake, writing in which I can see broader aspects of society or humanity. I do not want to love only one kind of literature—for example, only literature that announces its social importance as such, for I also love the hermetic, the private voices, intimate whispers that seem paradoxically to touch something universal in our souls. Still, what does it mean to be touched, as we say, by particular language? What does it mean to be *moved*? Our metaphors for reading imply changes of situation, changes of relationship. This book is an exploration of such changes, an effort to describe literary values so that, hopefully, they will not be forgotten in our rush to judgment.

We call some works of art powerful, but what do we mean by that power? The ancient Greeks knew the powers of the arts very well. The Theatre of Dionysus in Athens sat on a slope of the Acropolis, facing toward the south and the sea, so the audience would have seen not only the spectacle presented to them on the dancing floor but also the natural world of which their city was a part. I remember teaching Sophocles' *Antigone* in Athens in the spring of 2002. My small band of students and I had arrived in the city during Easter Week, when many citizens had left to spend the holidays in their ancestral villages, so the streets were spookily empty. We wandered through the Plaka, a neighborhood uncharacteristically devoid of tourists, and found a small empty square near a taverna named after its plane tree. There I asked my students to perform their prepared excerpts from the play.

As they read, enjoying the drama and their own performances, I experienced something of an epiphany. I was thinking of my country's turn toward a dangerous nationalism following 9/11, my alarm at the way religious conservatism was devouring societies all over the globe. We had arrived by sea after two weeks in Turkey, a country caught in the same struggle between fundamentalism and secular freedom. But wasn't Antigone, the heroine of Sophocles' play, a religious conservative? After all, her desire was simply to perform the funeral rites for her dead brothers, who had (like terrorists?) attacked the city. The play, I told my students, concerned many questions, among them the very idea of a city—in this case Thebes, standing in for Athens—a civilization, a culture, and ideas of authority or power over that city. What is a people, and how are they to be governed? What kind of power should we honor most—that of the ostensibly secular leader, Creon, or that of a young woman willing to die for her beliefs? From at least one point of view, the play inverts my liberal expectations and sympathies, asks me to feel the power of essential questions and the fatal freedom of its heroine. Literature teaches me that politics oversimplifies everything; love does not. And life confirms these lessons.

Now, I told my students, look where you are. Sunlight descended the bare, cracked walls of old houses. Birds twittered in the plane tree. The traffic seemed to have gone silent. This is Athens, I said, the city in which the play was first performed. We can walk a short distance to the ruins of the very theater in which it was staged. We can see the city and the sea, the realms of men and gods, and behold how poetic drama sings its vibrating chords between them. This is a particular kind of literary experience—not a newspaper column or a diatribe or a tract, but an engine of ambiguity, rage and grief and desperate heroism. Did *Antigone* or any other play of Sophocles change Athens? Did it end slavery in the city, improve the lives of women, create justice? Certainly not. But it brought its audience to a pitch of emotional insight, became one of the many mirrors in which they could see images of their lives.

Many years later, in 1971, when the great modern Greek poet George Seferis was carried to his grave and his funeral procession became a protest against Greece's fascist dictatorship, an actress stood at the graveside and recited lines from *Antigone* about the freedom of the individual conscience. Protests against fascism did not bring down that corrupt government by themselves, but they contributed to its downfall, and they were inspired at least in part by poetry.

So far, I have used the term "literature" rather broadly. Clearly, I have a hierarchy of values in mind. Some literary works are better than others, I have always said. Then I get stuck defining my terms and have to give specific examples. The essays here comprise a partial response.

As this book comes together, the world is particularly troubled—political division, war, extreme economic inequality, misogyny and racism, the threat of climate change and pandemic. Few of these problems are new. They need to be faced, and no doubt the many-headed thing we call literature, like all the arts, will play a complicated part in our human responses. But whether literature can result in justice of a more immediate kind, can help to modify police behavior or make automatic weapons more difficult to acquire or tax laws more equitable—well, the change we find in literary writing may be of a different quality and magnitude.

Consider another ancient Greek drama, the *Oresteia* of Aeschylus. Here the audience (predominantly male, most scholars agree) is harrowed by the spectacle of human violence and retribution. Before the first play in the trilogy opens, Agamemnon has sacrificed his daughter, Iphigenia, to make possible his invasion of Troy. He is then killed by his enraged wife, Clytemnestra, who is in turn killed by their son, Orestes. These offences (and generations of such offences in the House of Atreus) have fouled the very universe with gore. Spirits of the earth hound Orestes for his guilt, demanding justice, and finally that strange virgin goddess, Athena, faces another god, Apollo, along with the humans and the demons, in a court of law. Should Orestes die as his mother died?

Athena makes a preposterous argument concerning patriarchy—Orestes is not really his mother's son, since the male seed is the true progenitor (the woman is just a vessel, a repository), so his crime was not matricide. This seems frankly crazy, and modern readers are left to suppose that it merely upholds Athenian notions of patriarchy. But that is not all. Athena dictates that the dark, vengeful forces hounding Orestes will always have a place in the earth beneath the city and will never be forgotten. They are foundational and undeniable. Athena's justice is an injustice—no longer an eye for an eye, but an insistence that the violence must stop and people must live in peace with their own natures. We might say Athena chooses mercy over justice, and her patriarchal argument is little more than an excuse to stop the chain of murders. Yes, we complain, the patriarchy is left intact. Yes, the feminine Eumenides are now more or less out of sight, but they should never be out of mind, and the inadequacy, the *problem* of Athena's justice, will be enshrined in the city.

To the Greeks, it seems to me, ideal justice is not achievable; it always creates another injustice. Human beings are by themselves unable to stop the endless cycle of killing and revenge, but a goddess can step in and say, "Enough. Stop this ridiculous nonsense." That is Athena's role—just as it is at the end of Homer's *Odyssey*, when Odysseus combats the families of the suitors he has killed. We are left with a sobering vision of human potential—not entirely unhopeful, but not really comforting either.

Readers who want works of literature to offer immediate and unquestioning justice are reading naively, missing the very contradiction and complexity of human nature, which has not changed all that much since the time of the ancients. As my favorite Australian poet, Cally Conan-Davies, has written, "Mayhem and metamorphosis / is what the old gods promised us." We should listen to those old gods as well as our more modern, aspirational voices. Our efforts at justice must find, somewhere, such virtues as kindness and, where possible, forgiveness, empathy, and what James Joyce called "restless living wounding doubt."

PERHAPS CHANGE HAPPENS in more ways than we know. "You must change your life," the poet Rainer Maria Rilke said. And if we have experienced such a change, such a fire of transformation when we felt we would surely die and yet we came through it more or less intact, we might imagine understanding what the poet meant. Rilke says that we are *seen* and that being seen is part of the change. Think of loving another person, really seeing that person, allowing their history to be what it is, and you might understand how you and the beloved are both changed by recognition. We often speak of seeing images of ourselves in books, but we also see images of others. We don't learn moral virtue so much as the range of human possibilities, good and bad, ways in which people behave and express or fail to express themselves. We don't *agree* with literary texts so much as *live* them.

Seeing and being seen are important and intimate matters. I live in Tasmania now, the island state of Australia, at roughly the same latitude south as my birthplace was latitude north, but on the other side of the world, in a more watery hemisphere. I live by another clock, another calendar. I live without most of the possessions acquired in my American life, including a large library that had to be abandoned when I moved. I do, in many ways, feel translated, re-embodied, made new even as I age. Perhaps this is what young John Keats meant by "Dying into life," or what Yeats intended when he wrote, "Many times man lives and dies / Between his two eternities." These deaths in life, these sheddings of old skin, are nothing more than our participation in the book of the world, a book you never read the same way twice. I have the feeling that how we say a thing matters, as when Philip Larkin calls life "this frail / Travelling coincidence." A lifetime's plays and novels reside in that one phrase. Larkin depicts an ordinary world of weddings seen from a train. The seeing and the saying are transformational, as he avers about this life: ". . . and what it held / Stood ready to be loosed with all the power / That being changed can give."

What is this "being changed"? He's not talking about winning the lottery or buying a new car, but a change at the level of soul and being, an enlargement before a diminuendo, the way we measure our most consequential days. Real eloquence is a high achievement, helpful even when we fail to parse it. Words for delight, words for living. Words that matter, that cut through the drivel and noise of the world.

And seeing, really seeing, really hearing, really being alive to the senses, is the beginning of the connections we make in art. As we live in our bodies, so we read the world. This is what I mean by my title, *Incarnation & Metamorphosis*, embodiment and change.

I was sitting on the bank of a river in Tasmania—there's a sentence for you! I was sixty-five years old, enjoying a day without the pressure of work, looking out at the light of marshlands and the tilting flight of a plover, when I noticed movement in the muddy bank below me. Tiny crabs had come out of holes in the mud and were feeding, or at least prodding the wet with the picks of their little legs. When I stood to look at them, I must have loomed too much, and they scampered instantly back into their holes. So I sat and waited without moving, and soon they came out again. I stood and they disappeared. I had thought *I saw them*, assumed my seeing was paramount in this universe. But they saw me, too, or sensed me, and responded. We human beings are noticed more than we know. We are seen. And literature, too, is telling us that we are seen, warts and all. Criticism, such as the essays in this book, is a way of seeing back.

Literature educates the whole person, body and soul, compelling us through experiences where explanations are difficult if not impossible, asking us to live with uncertainty and doubt, to understand that meaning is rarely one thing. As John Devitt used to say, meaning is a "field of possibilities." John's friend Seamus Heaney once noted in an interview how poetry had taught him "That there's such a thing as truth and it can be told—slant; that subjectivity is not to be theorized away and is worth defending; that poetry itself has virtue. . . ." Heaney alludes to Emily Dickinson. Writers speak to each other across time, and this, too, is one of the virtues of literature, really of all the arts. It is like the world looking back at us.

The primary goal of my writing, like that of my teaching over thirty years, has been to defend the "thisness" of literary works, their very particularity, the *way* they happen and the freedom they offer the honest heart. Insisting that literary works toe anyone's political line is not freedom, nor is attacking the human beings who made them. The rush to judgment must be resisted. Literature asks us to slow down, take pleasure in the words that make us who we are, and hopefully be more aware of the planet on which we are privileged to live.

I begin with incarnation, embodiment, because literature means through the body, not just as it slumps in a reading chair, but also as it dances and acts. The process of metamorphosis—a very real phenomenon in nature—reminds us that we do change, we do shed our skins, die and find ourselves reborn. I have often stirred memoir into literary criticism in the belief that we are always telling stories, no matter what genre we adopt. This is how we face each other and try to say what we enjoy and why, and what we believe and why. I love George Orwell when he says, "To write in plain, vigorous language, one has to think fearlessly, and if one thinks fearlessly,

one cannot be politically orthodox." We have enough orthodoxy in this world. Let's try to shake it up a little.

A FEW OF THESE ESSAYS began as book reviews or served other
purposes before being reworked. I would like to thank the editors of the periodicals in which they first appeared, including
*The Dark Horse, The Hudson Review, Literary Matters, The Los
Angeles Review of Books, The Sewanee Review, The Wall Street
Journal,* and *The Woven Tale Press.* My thanks extend as well to
the staff at Paul Dry Books.

Tasmania, December 2021

PART ONE

The Way
of Literature

Incarnation &
Metamorphosis

AN ESSAY IN METAPHORS

1. My Theory of Language

Two propositions: 1) To be embodied is to change. 2) Literature, as a form of embodiment, is both incarnation and metamorphosis.

Literature begins in the beginning with absence, the damned white page, the writer as a nervy little god governing and being governed by creation. So we summon our metaphors for the act of making, whether from nothing or from something else. Darkness on the face of the deep, then a flash of light— an unfolding into being, or covalence and dividing cells. As Ovid's *Metamorphoses* put it (in Charles Martin's translation):

> Now when the god (whichever one it was)
> had given Chaos form, dividing it
> in parts which he arranged, he molded earth
> into the shape of an enormous globe. . . .

Which god was it, anyway? Ovid's characteristic whimsy is a useful response to what appears unknowable—it started *some-*

where, somehow. In moments of embodiment, receiving signals from our telltale senses, we begin using words. The poem or story bodies forth. "And the word was made flesh and dwelt among us," says the Gospel of John, which equates the beginning with the word, a metaphor projecting its meaning in multiple directions. John the Baptist, the preacher-poet depicted in the first chapter of the gospel, "was not that Light, but was sent to bear witness of that Light." Writers are like that: go-betweens, mediums, hermetic bearers of the news that stays news. Writers are strange primitives who still believe in incantations and spells, words remembering worlds. In the Bible the word is incarnation with all its ambiguity, its witnesses, mysteries of interpretation and understanding.

I have a rather whimsical theory of language—probably close to Freud's theory of language, too. It goes like this:

In the beginning was the womb, a warm sea. That was our being, our unity, our oneness, an Eden without other animals requiring names, and a darkness upon the face of the deep. Plugged into the Mother Ship, we were, if lucky, nourished and perfectly loved. We were creatures of an amniotic sea who would ever after yearn for the other, larger sea, but as yet we knew nothing of desire, nothing of language except those coos from the other side, those musical phrases being sung to us, those other skins rubbing outside our walls of skin. As our fins became hands and feet, we dwelt incarnate, unthinking, blissed out.

Then something happened. Some universal fault line shivered and the earth moved and the sea shuddered and our world broke open. Everything was strain and struggle. Someone was screaming, and it might have been us or it might have been Mother. In rapid succession our bellies were severed from Mother, our bottoms were slapped, our throats were cleared and we began to scream. It was cold. Something we would later call *air* became very important to us—we drank great gulps of it like eaters of wind, farting and burping the residue. We discovered wetness and were not sure it was good. There was a lot of blood and the moods of the air were anxiously happy.

Nothing could solve our problems but a breast, and (again if we were lucky) the breast soon came, and fingers squeezing milk into our madly sucking mouths. The universal good of nipple and skin. The Mother Ship, if indeed this was Mother, the imprint of skin, the smell and taste of survival, which we took greedily into our mouths and would later call love.

We had fingers and toes and various ways of evacuating bowels and bladder, and such malleable skulls and hair or no hair and eyes that had not yet discovered they were meant for seeing. There were other sounds now, sharper and colder sounds, but we had not felt terror and only made sounds when we wanted the breast.

When the breast went away we screamed. Or we slept, sated and warm. Then we woke and screamed and the breast came back and we made sounds like pigeons on a window sill, though of course we had no idea of pigeons yet. We only knew absence and touch, absence and touch, cold and warm, not-skin and skin. And skin was better than not-skin.

Our sounds were a chaos, a caterwaul. They were rarely cute, but the faces still smiled on us at least occasionally, and we began to recognize them. The breasts had a face too, the best face of all (if we were lucky) filled with a look we could never understand, a look that made it possible for us to find nourishment and begin to use our fingers and toes in unaccustomed ways.

When that face and those breasts went away, language was born. It might have been a syllable such as *Ma!* Notice the smacking of lips when you say it. Some amount of time elapses, though, before the face with the breasts has been trained to respond to our language. Signification comes with significance.

In the beginning was the word, and the word might have been *Ma!* It might have been *Gah!* or *Bah!* Or *Ba-ba!* But it was a word and it got results. Syllables came when the breast was removed and the mouth was not otherwise occupied. Our first delight in syllables had nothing to do with meaning, only with sound and oral pleasure and necessity.

Language was born in absence. It is a symptom of estrangement, and it becomes a key part of our impossible journey back to the womb, the remembered oneness, the Eden we have lost. And no matter what language we speak, we believe for a time in the magic of words, their ability to conjure and incarnate. People who do not lose that belief often become writers. We know, or think we know, that literary incarnations are not literal, but exist on a path parallel to the paths of actual human beings. We entertain belief in order to learn and especially to change. We need—I do, anyway—to be changed or moved from one location to another, or given a way of saying we have never heard before. Making, incarnating, is inseparable from changing.

2. The Laurel Tree

Learning a new language, one often has word-discoveries, epiphanies of origin. Greek, for example, gives one the pleasant sensation of touching original elements in words. The Gospel of John is full of fundamentals, like λόγον and ἐρημος— "word" and "desert" (or "wilderness" in the KJV). You spell them out and begin to understand all the "ologies" and "eremites" of English. Many years ago, shopping for herbs and spices in Greece, I found myself examining a packet of bay leaves. Δάφνη, the packet said. Daphne. The word made flesh, the flesh turned into a tree, its leaves potentially flavoring my food. A poet wears the bay, the laurel crown, and the story of the laurel lies at the very source of poetry in the West.

"My mind leads me to speak now," Ovid says, "of forms changed / into new bodies. . . ." In his version of the story, Daphne was the daughter of Peneus, a river god, and in the beginning she lived quite happily on her own. Unfortunately, due to Cupid's devilry, the god Apollo fell in love with her.

Pierced by one of Cupid's gold-tipped arrows, Apollo, like a drunken frat boy on spring break, had to possess the beautiful girl, and his pursuit could only end disastrously.

> . . . the young god had no further interest
> in wasting his fine words on her; admonished
> by his own passion, he accelerates,
> and runs as swiftly as a Gallic hound
> chasing a rabbit through an open field. . . .

The switch to present tense in Martin's translation comes like a change of gears in a god-machine bearing down on the innocent creature of flesh. The simile is important—metaphor is metamorphosis, moving from one form to another. I am reminded of the living dog meeting a dead one in the "Proteus" chapter of Joyce's *Ulysses*:

> The dog yelped running to them, reared up and pawed them, dropping on all fours, again reared up at them with mute bearish fawning. Unheeded he kept by them as they came up towards the drier sand, a rag of wolf's tongue redpanting from his jaws. His speckled body ambled ahead of them and then loped off at a calf's gallop. The carcass lay on his path. He stopped, sniffed, stalked round it, brother, nosing closer, went round it, sniffing rapidly like a dog all over the dead dog's bedraggled fell. Dogskull, dogsniff, eyes on the ground, moves to one great goal. Ah, poor dogsbody! Here lies poor dogsbody's body.

Joyce, who had Ovid very much in mind, would later make a verbal play on "dog" and "God," who "becomes man becomes fish becomes barnacle goose becomes featherbed mountain." Metaphor is metamorphosis. The dog is a wolf and a bear and a cow as it sorts out just what it means to be dead or alive, and even God, whatever that word signifies, must have many forms.

Metamorphosis is a sort of reincarnation, re-embodiment after a sleep. As Yeats put it, "Many times man lives and dies / Between his two eternities." We have never been one thing, from our development in the womb to our recycled cells throughout life and our many psychic deaths. The many-shaped god pursuing Daphne did not yet realize, or forgot in the heat of his pursuit, that she too could be changed. He did not see her as a living, separate being, but as the manifestation of his own desire. Daphne was desperate to save herself in more ways than one. She wanted not just to avoid being raped, but also to preserve her autonomy, her very nature. So she cried out, "'Help me, dear father! If your waters hold / divinity, transform me and destroy / that beauty by which I have too well pleased!'"

The myth's gendered nature is devastatingly precise. How many women have found themselves in Daphne's place, trying to escape the blind, possessive lust of an Apollo?

In describing her transformation, Martin's translation again switches from past to present tense, from storytelling to immediate experience:

> Her prayer was scarcely finished when she feels
> a torpor take possession of her limbs—
> her supple trunk is girdled with a thin
> layer of fine bark over her smooth skin;
> her hair turns into foliage, her arms
> grow into branches, sluggish roots adhere
> to feet that were so recently so swift,
> her head becomes the summit of a tree;
> all that remains of her is a warm glow.

Is this Daphne's nature in another form? Is her escape a triumph or a catastrophe? When the rivers gather they are "uncertain whether to congratulate, / or to commiserate with Daphne's father. . . ." The change is a terrible necessity, and the god refuses to accept defeat. Apollo plucks a branch of the laurel tree to weave his crown, the very laurel crown that will be bestowed upon kings, generals, and poets, signifying victory in competition or laureateship. Ovid tells us that Daphne assents to this, but surely the residue of anguish lingers. Anyone who has seen Bernini's miraculous statue of Apollo and Daphne in Rome will understand how the anguish lingers. I have seen marble weep, and I have seen someone I loved gazing on that statue, moved to tears. Think of that cliché phrase— moved to tears—and you will again participate in the mysteries of art, of incarnation and metamorphosis.

Remember Daphne when you cook your spaghetti sauce and write your poems. Remember her passion, struggle, and change.

3. The Given Fire

So runs my odd family romance of poetry and desire, language and skin, motion and emotion. Metamorphosis is incarnation. Incarnation is metamorphosis. Out of something, something else. So many stories use birth as the essence and metaphor of creation. In the "Theogony" of Apollodorus, for example, Ouranos (Heaven) marries Ge (Earth), and fathers creatures called the Hundred-Handers, named for their multiplying bodies. Given the permutations of life forms on our planet, this hardly seems extreme. We can even imagine what it might be like to dance like Shiva with so many arms.

Our bodies are the instruments on which we play our words, and with the same instruments we express our desires and animosities. We suffer because of these desires and animosities, and at times our life on earth seems a trial to us. We may try to leave the earth, or escape its gravitational pull, but escape raises the question of return. When Robert Frost imagines climbing a birch tree toward heaven, he next imagines the birch bending and putting him back on earth, which is "the right place for love," because on earth we have bodies to express our love with. And we have both trouble and poetry because of these bodies.

Poetry is not made of ideals, but of words. Even in tidy measures, it has a rebellious heart, and it resists purifying abstraction. In "Plato, or Why," the great Polish poet Wisława Szymborska wrote,

> For unclear reasons
> under unknown circumstances
> Ideal Being ceased to be satisfied.
>
> It could have gone on forever,
> hewn from darkness, forged from light,
> in its sleepy gardens above the world.
>
> Why on earth did it start seeking thrills
> in the bad company of matter?
>
> (Clare Cavanagh and Stanislaw Baranezak, trans.)

There's a bit of anarchy, a romance of bodily imperfection, even in the most exacting writing.

Poets often speak about the desire for escape from bodily suffering—Keats, Yeats, and Frost leap to mind—but generally they return to the quotidian. Body is instrument, incarnation is both subject and object. Mary Shelley suggested that we are all in some sense Frankenstein's monster—creatures forged by some Promethean figure from the parts (or DNA) of other creatures, learning to move, learning language. That's why we love Caliban, who wakes and cries to dream again— we recognize him in ourselves. We make things out of necessity, but also because we are made things ourselves, monsters who learn to talk and write. Shelley's novel reminds us that Prometheus created us by mixing water and earth. He brought us fire, hidden in the stalk of a fennel.

I love that detail of the fennel stalk as much as I love creation's Hundred-Handers. Writers can be Darwins of the fantastic—observing the constantly-changing world, recording marvelous data. But we are also shapers—the Greek word for poetry means "construction" or "making." Prometheus made us of mud and gave us fire. We need to be burned by that fire in order to know it and, in our own Promethean gesture, give it to others. The metamorphosis cannot be only a subject of literature. It must also be a goal. Whether as readers or writers, we want to be changed, or at least moved, by the poem or story. Both readers and writers want to burn, and also to be doused in the waters of change.

Once, strolling through the town of Stromness in Orkney—the islands off the north coast of Scotland—I saw the marvelous poet George Mackay Brown out for his evening walk. I was too shy to introduce myself and tell him how much I admired his work. But as we passed each other in the cobbled street, he looked my way and smiled—his long-jawed face and gray hair giving him a mythical appearance. He could have been a fisherman or a crewman for Erik the Red. Mackay Brown's poetry is infused with Orkney's Viking accents and its Scottish dialect. Stromness was once called Hamnavoe, and his poem of that name, resurrecting the word in memory, is as much a statement of poetics as anything he wrote. "Hamnavoe" is a poem of appreciation for his father, who delivered letters. It follows the father on his postal route, taking note of the community and its history as he passes. It also honors the man's work, which like a poet's carries words from one person to others. The poem ends as follows:

The kirk, in a gale of psalms, went heaving through
A tumult of roofs, freighted for heaven. And lovers
Unblessed by steeples lay under
The buttered bannock of the moon.

He quenched his lantern, leaving the last door.
Because of his gay poverty that kept
My seapink innocence
From the worm and the black wind;

And because, under equality's sun,
All things wear now to a common soiling,
In the fire of images
Gladly I put my hand
To save that day for him.

The fire is the hurtful knowledge that comes of experience, but also the images by which we understand or relive it. This fire burns in a world of vanishings and metamorphoses. The rain-wet stones of Hamnavoe will outlast the town's inhabitants, perhaps even outlast the poems of its greatest writer, yet who can say the day has not been saved?

2019

At Home in the Imaginal

I'M THINKING OF a library, a treasury of human thoughts and imaginings, mappings, descriptions, blunders, desires, the kind you walk into, sit down in, touch the spines of books in, smelling the paper and ink, noticing the other denizens who all seem to be focused on something other than themselves. Every book, every article, map, or film in this library came from the minds of other human beings, from all over the globe and many different points in time. It is more than we will ever learn ourselves. We can reach into these books and find the lives of others and discover how little human beings have changed since the time of Homer, yet also how various we are, how colorful in our skin tones and genders and languages and cultures. What a privilege it is to join you in this library and talk about a few things I love, as I love the freedom of imagination, as I love books and sometimes even the people who made them.

Most of the books in this library take part in a very human activity, storytelling, and look at all the ways in which one can

This essay was first delivered as a "Last Lecture" at The Colorado College, a few months before my retirement from teaching.

tell a story, from a poem to a mathematical theorem to a narrative of rocks and snow to a map. Story comes from everywhere. And all of these things feed the imagination, the very quality that makes us human and helps us find connections in life. We are here to grow our capacity to tell stories. This capacity, which you can tend like a gardener, is what I call imagination, and without it our lives would be much diminished, even impossible.

Imagination is sometimes associated with untruth, but imagination is true—at least as true as memory, as Thomas Hobbes reminds us in *Leviathan* or Tim O'Brien dramatizes in "How to Tell a True War Story." Any time we try to tell a story, we learn again the reality, the inevitability, of the imaginal, to use a word coined by the philosopher and Islamist Henry Corbin, who wanted to honor this human quality without descending into triviality. He was thinking partly about story and connection, stories that make connections. So am I.

Once, some twenty years ago in Greece, I had an encounter that could have happened in Homer.

I was strolling through a village, Kastania, high in the Taygetos Mountains of the southern Peloponnese. It was spring, the village fountains overflowing with snowmelt, the water gushing down the streets and paths, so walking on stones felt like wading in a stream. The world was flowing. Greek mountain villages are wealthy in water, their cisterns keeping it cool even in the hottest summer months, and to see so much of it flowing freely, profligately away somehow lightened the spirit. The village was alive with water.

I was looking for a church whose frescoes were reported to be very fine, and only when I stood on the hillside across the village from it could I make out the little bell tower above the tiled rooftops. High up in the mountains the rocks form a kind of theater. You can hear the voices of villagers chattering from house to house, the goat bells climbing the mountainside, the monosyllabic shouts of the goatherds prodding their flocks.

Crossing the village, suddenly I lost sight of the church's bell tower. My angle of vision had changed, and I could no longer see so clearly. I paced in a lane below where I thought it should stand, looking up at the houses, trying to remember where the bell tower had risen. An old man came toward me up the lane. His silver hair and mustache were neatly trimmed, and he wore clean western clothes, perhaps having come from some business in one of the villages down by the sea. I greeted him in the customary way, and he returned my greeting. Then he asked, *"Pou pas?"*

It was a common question to ask of a stranger. *Where are you going?* He asked it as much with a turn of one wrist as with his words.

I explained what I was looking for, the old church with the frescoes.

"Einai píso," he said. "It's behind." He pointed to a wall with a gate. *"Éla."* Come.

His name was Nikos. He was in his seventies, but nimble as one of his goats. I followed him through that latched gate into another world.

These were Nikos's goat pens, situated between his house and the village lane. They were crudely built, with spaces between the boards admitting sunlight on the straw where a dozen suckling kids bleated and scampered about. We walked bent over under the rusty metal roof, our eyes adjusting to the dark, then emerged into sunlight in a yard of packed dirt and grass tufts under a plane tree.

I felt as if I had walked through a tunnel back in time. There stood Nikos's wife, Fotiní, dressed in her workaday rags and headscarf. She had been feeding the chickens from a bowl of scraps in her red hands. Nikos introduced us. He directed me to take a seat on a stump in the yard while Fotiní went to get food for the stranger.

"Are you married?" Nikos asked me.

"Yes," I said.

"Do you have children?"

"I have a daughter." Stepdaughter. It was complicated, but I kept my story simple.

Nikos sat near me on a block of wood. He touched my arm. "Well," he said, "did you steal your wife or did she steal you?"

"She stole my heart," I said.

Fotiní had been making *mizíthra*, the mild white cheese, and she emerged from the house with a bowl of warm, yogurty stuff and some bread rusks, an elemental meal for the stranger, who in Greek culture is also a guest.

"I stole her," Nikos said of his wife.

"From her father?"

"Yes!" He cackled, slapping his knee, while Fotiní stood by, blushing, looking pleased with his story.

They had relatives in America, Chicago, but had never been. We sat under fresh goatskins hung to dry from a branch of the plane tree. Nikos opened a spigot under the tree and filled three glasses with the freshest water I have ever tasted. This was how they greeted me, with conversation and food. They could be Baucis and Philemon, I thought—the story from the Roman poet, Ovid, of the pious couple who care for two strangers, not knowing the strangers are gods in disguise. Or this could be a scene in Homer, this simple act of kindness and curiosity, Odysseus welcomed by the Phaeacians. This is the culture of *philoxenía* so common in the eastern Mediterranean. One treats the stranger well, enlarging one's own spirit in doing so.

We sat in the yard for perhaps an hour, talking of our lives. Nikos was the oldest of twelve brothers. Of his own four children, only one remained in the village, now tending the goats on the mountainside for the summer months. They would join the son, camping in the high country, when the suckling goats were stronger, sleeping under the stars with their flock. "The young are leaving us," Nikos said. Once there were two thousand people in the village, now only one hundred fifty. But, said Fotiní, they had ten grandchildren, which was a good thing.

"Tell your wife she must give you a son," Nikos said.

I let it pass. It was not my place, I felt at the time, to disagree or explain my complicated life. And it was no time to argue about overpopulation, global warming, or any of the other concerns that weigh upon us now. This was a gentle meeting of very different people in a spirit of kindness and curiosity. In the same spirit, I invite you not to worry whether or not the story is true. It's a memory, which means it is partly or wholly composed of imagination—images. Nikos opened the church for me, let me gaze on the frescoes, faded and moldy with time, darkened by candle smoke. I was curious about them as art, curious about the masterful iconography of devils and monsters, the local stories from another time. But there was also a gulf between this old agrarian and me, as if we inhabited different planets and were only catching glimpses of each other. We could only go so far in our connection. If I were to imagine Nikos as a character in a novel, or if he or Fotiní were inclined to imagine me, we might go much further, but not as ourselves—we would be imaginal beings, translated, given new coherence that we may not possess in a literal biography. The character Nikos and the man Nikos would never be the same thing. Living in story always means that we are living in more than one way.

Many horrible things have been done in the name of religion in villages like Kastania, and many beautiful things as well, such as the kindness shown to a stranger. The village was said to have supported the fascists in the Greek Civil War that erupted after the Nazi occupation. Maybe so. Was Nikos a fascist? Was his father a fascist? As his guest, I was not about to ask, and for the time being it did not matter. I had evidence of his old-fashioned belief in patriarchy, but really knew nothing about his politics. Despite our differences, we had met, we had enjoyed each other's company for a little while. I had tasted water, fried bread, and new cheese from the milk of this kindly couple's goats. Their spirit of civility relates to what I mean by imagination, a realm in which we can see another without feeling that the other has to be changed right here, right now, into a more perfect person. It's a willingness to hear another person's story without having to correct it or elevate oneself above it in moral superiority.

This is something like the way we meet a character in a novel. We know the character is invented, yet we entertain the reality of that person almost as we would a figure in real life. We judge, but we also suspend judgment in our effort to understand, to see the life of another. I don't read books in order to validate myself, but to expand the boundaries of my experience. And I write for the same reason, whether from my own or from other points of view. I want more life, and I want to hold it more beautifully up to the light before it vanishes. To see the humanity of a man like Nikos, a woman like Fotiní, without knowing a thing about their politics or how rigidly old-fashioned they may or may not be is to make unexpected connections, to learn about compassion as well as judgment, to widen one's circle of life. The moment lives, both in and out of time, as a story.

The poet Seamus Heaney once wrote, quoting Coventry Patmore, "The end of art is peace." I thought of the line in Kastania on that peaceful spring day in the mountains of melting snow. Stories teach us that we are all caught in the same tragedy, we all die searching for meaning, hearing secret harmonies or hoping to hear them. That is why *philoxenía*, the kindness to strangers, matters so much, and why the free imagination keeps us from being quite the monsters we might otherwise be.

MENTION OF AN Irish poet like Heaney calls to mind another story of hospitality. This happened to me many years ago in Belfast, Northern Ireland. It was 1975, the height of the Troubles. I was a twenty-year-old hitchhiker, living on money I had made unloading fishing boats in Alaska. My mother country was Scotland, my mother tongue English, and my travels on foot through the isles were a magic immersion in language, a confirmation of vocation and love.

Someone gave me the name of an American living in Belfast and said if I went to the city the American could put me up for the night. So I took the train from Dublin and gave the American's address to a cabbie in Belfast and was taken through the streets to a hillside neighborhood. The cab departed and I walked up the steps of a row house across from a park. The neighborhood, I later learned, was Protestant, with tidy brick houses and trim little yards in the spring sunlight. After some time ringing the bell of the American's house and getting no answer, I crossed to the park, where children played and a few old pensioners sat on benches. Watching the old men in their silences and their stories, perhaps I remembered lines by my favorite Irish poet, William Butler Yeats:

Though lads are making pikes again
For some conspiracy,
And crazy rascals rage their fill
At human tyranny,
My contemplations are of Time
That has transfigured me.

Yeats was in his twenties when he imagined that wild old man, and I was in my teens when I first read him. I was the sort of boy who always connected life and art, mixing them up, feeling the way art lives in time and out of it, just like the human mind and imagination.

That day in Belfast I learned a few more things. I learned a British Army stockade hunkered just up the street between that Protestant neighborhood and the Catholic area higher on the hillside. The stockade was prickly with barbed wire and automatic rifles, and every now and then it released a squad on patrol, guns pointing fore and aft as they walked the streets. I had naively wandered into a war zone. No one could tell me where the American had gone. He apparently worked for a church organization trying to get Protestant and Catholic kids to meet each other and overcome their ancient, tribal animosities. I could feel, talking to children in the park and to some of the old pensioners in their dark suits, a certain good will edged with a certain tension, a wariness about this American boy standing lost among them, a knapsack on his back.

I spent the whole day in that park, except when I excused myself to wander uphill and look at the Catholic houses, which were smaller, dimmer, more shuttered and silent. They were an unspoken bitterness. I remember one small corner shop with very few goods on the shelves, how nervous I felt when the soldiers emerged from their prickly stockade and I returned to the serene enclosure of the park. A small boy and girl wanted me to play with them, and we ran about a green hillside, the two of them chattering like birds. A great house flying a flag could be seen in the distance, and the little girl called it "God's Castle." They lived in their own empire of imagination, even in that troubled space. Later that afternoon I met the father of these two children. He was home from work and collecting them for tea, a thin young man with a kindly face, like all the others very curious to meet this young American hitchhiker. It was he who told me, while his children tugged at his hands for attention, that the other American, the one I had come to Belfast to meet, was away on the continent at one of his church camps, and would not be back for days.

Now the old pensioners and the park keeper in his blue uniform and cap decided they must help me out. One of them gave me sandwiches he had brought for his day in the park, buttered white bread and ham. They would be closing the gate at nightfall. They were worried for my safety.

The white-haired keeper had an office, a sort of garden shed with a concrete floor, a stove, table, and chair, and he said I could sleep there for the night. He would lock me in for my own safety—night was a dangerous time—and another keeper would spring me loose in the morning. Meanwhile, there was a little fire in the stove and a tea kettle, and I had the sandwiches. I had a foam pad and sleeping bag in my knapsack, a few changes of clothes and some books. I was also rather stupidly lugging a portable typewriter in a case, having decided I was a writer.

I spent that night alone, locked in the park keeper's hut, with a cup of tea and sandwiches for my evening meal. There was a kerosene lamp I could stand on the floor by my sleeping bag, so I propped my head on my knapsack pillow and read. The book I was reading, a Penguin paperback, was Ernest Hemingway's *For Whom the Bell Tolls*, about the civil war in Spain, and I was gripped by it.

There is nothing like immersion in a novel, particularly when you are young. On ships in Alaska I had read *Moby Dick* and *War and Peace*. On the road in Britain, Ireland, and the continent I would read Malcolm Lowry's *Under the Volcano*, Joyce's *Portrait of the Artist as a Young Man*, assorted books by Hemingway, Oscar Wilde, Chekhov, and then one glorious week in Spain I would finish *Anna Karenina*. I'm not sure it matters so much which books I was reading. What matters is the degree to which I was able to grow my imaginative capacities, to feel deeply the importance of language and story and the connection of these things to the world in which I walked.

That night in Belfast, I would later learn, there was a murder, an execution really. But I knew nothing of it and read on, a bit nervous in the park keeper's hut but eventually able to sleep on the concrete floor. Due to the kindness of some old men who knew nothing about me, I was safe.

In the morning a key turned in the lock, the door swung open and a new keeper appeared with an apple for my breakfast. The old men were gathering for a morning in the park. One had news of the killing in the night. I decided I had better leave, thanked all the people who had cared for me and shouldered my pack. Downhill from the park I found a cab being shared by four others—cabs often took more than one fare, a practical adjustment in an occupied city. We were heading down to the city's heart when a British Army roadblock pulled us over to inspect our luggage for bombs. The young soldier who examined my passport kept his automatic rifle pointed at my hiking boots. I did not understand the words he barked at me, but the cabbie took my arm and guided me back inside the car and we were off.

"Yer an American?" the cabbie asked.

I told him I was and gave him the name of the other American I had wanted to meet.

"I know him," the cabbie said as he drove. "I'll take you to another fella knows him." Thus began another strange day in Belfast, and as I write I find myself scrambling to remember details—the cab driver's face, which I would have seen only in glimpses, given my shyness and my case of nerves, the faces of the other passengers in the car, the number of soldiers at the roadblock, the names of streets as we entered the city center. I was lost, completely in the hands of others, and damned lucky those others had no malevolent designs. Neighborhoods went by in the window, some with deserted streets, some thronged with traffic. Passengers were unloaded until I was the last remaining. Finally we stopped in a near-empty street of small, cheerless row houses. "Here's your man."

I hefted my knapsack and typewriter, stood behind the cabbie as he rapped on the door of a narrow house.

The door teetered off its hinges and fell inward against the entry wall.

"Jaysus!"

We peered inside a bare parlor where a man lay on the floor in a sleeping bag. He was just sitting up, rubbing his eyes at the light.

"The fuck happened to yer door?"

The man on the floor was young, rumpled, hungover. He squinted at us and explained that paratroopers had butted down the door in a house-to-house search and he hadn't bothered to fix the hinges. "They'll just knock it down again."

The cabbie introduced me as an American looking for an American and I might need looking after. Before I knew it he was gone and I was helping the hungover young man place the door back on its hinges.

After forty-five years I have forgotten his name. I remember the smell of beer and cigarettes in his little parlor, but not why he was sleeping on the floor instead of a room upstairs. I remember he had to pull on his trousers and button his shirt, and how he immediately set about trying to make me feel at home. Let's call him Sean. I would guess Sean was older than me by a few years. He was scrawny, with short dark hair. I knew nothing about the neighborhood where I had been dropped, nothing about its religious or economic make-up, only that Sean worked for the same church organization as my missing American. He earned about twenty pounds a week, enough to keep him fed and smoking.

Sean explained to me how the churches invited children from both tribes, Protestant and Catholic, to camps on the continent where they could meet and play and get to know each other. My American was there now and would be gone a few more days.

This is what I want to tell you about Sean, with whom that day I watched hours of an incomprehensible cricket match on a snowy black and white TV. I went with him on his cigarette run to a shop across the street, and on our return I shared a meal with him. He was very poor, but didn't seem to care. In back of his little parlor was a kitchen with an old cast iron stove and a gas ring for cooking. The stove no longer worked, so it had become his larder. When he opened the door I saw his food supply: a bowl of eggs, a loaf of bread and a fold of butcher's paper containing a few strips of bacon.

Sean cooked us a meal on the gas ring: eggs and bread with slabs of butter. And he gave me the bacon. I tried to share it with him, but he insisted. We ate our meal in silence before the snowy cricket match, a kind of benediction at the altar of the game.

A man who had nothing gave me all he had. I felt ashamed of my uselessness, my inability to understand even the game on the TV or the accents of the commentators.

There were other adventures in Belfast, some more menacing, but I tell this part of it now because of the way I was treated by strangers, the way I was watched and worried over, taken in, taken care of, fed. This care for the stranger enacted in real life seems to me related to stories, our care for the strangers in books. We have to give them something, our time and patience and curiosity, in order to receive their gifts of connection, drama, and insight. We have to make ourselves at home in stories, which means being at home in uncertainty, suspense, awkwardness, strangeness. Stories remind us that we are not always right and we can't know everything about other human beings. We can't change their natures, yet we must determine how we feel about them all the same. Stories are life.

"THE END OF ART is peace." But what trouble and turmoil it can give us along the way.

To be a reader is to invite that turmoil and uncertainty even as you search for beauty and connection. The greatest Irish poet, Yeats, is great in part because of the sheer range of human feelings his work expresses, the audacity of his foolishness as well as his wisdom, the muscularity and memorability of his technique. I love Yeats as an example even when I strongly disagree with him, and I think being able to reside with an artist in such complicated terms, the sort of love-hate one might experience in one's own family or any community, is a good thing, closer to real life than some purity of consensus might be. His willingness to express ugly emotions, wild ideas, the full reach of his imagination, is a kind of daring almost unheard of in any artist today. Yeats wasn't worried about Twitter or Facebook telling him he couldn't try, and he wouldn't have given a damn anyway. He wasn't an unfettered artist, but he chose his own fetters, and that's the only way a real artist can behave.

We can find Yeats being foolish in some statements about women, for example, but then there is his dynamic effort to really see and honor women very different from himself in "No Second Troy" and "Adam's Curse." We can see him denouncing Irish mediocrity and fecklessness in "September 1913": "Romantic Ireland's dead and gone. / It's with O'Leary in the grave." Then within a few years he admits his mistake, wrestling with the politics he had thought so destructive in what is arguably the greatest political poem ever written, "Easter 1916."

Political poetry often suffers from an oversimplification of experience. This is a great political poem because it remains uncertain of its truth, or even of the realm in which a political statement can be true. It wrestles with its being, its physics and metaphysics, as much as what it is saying.

It's hard to say where the Irish troubles began—with the Normans, the Vikings, the Elizabethans, Cromwell, or William of Orange. They came to a head in the nineteenth century on three fronts. There was the legal political process trying for Home Rule and property rights, led by the charismatic Charles Stewart Parnell. There were the various terrorist brotherhoods that would eventually form organizations like the IRA. And there was the cultural movement to re-animate an Irish identity, led by figures such as Yeats, Lady Gregory, and John Millington Synge. The Home Rule movement was defeated not by the British Empire as you might expect, but by Irish conservatives, puritanical Catholics who brought down Parnell because he was an adulterer. The martyrdom of Parnell is a major element in the fiction of Joyce and the poetry of Yeats. The fecklessness and ineptitude of Irish nationalists, all talk and no gravy, seemed impervious to change.

But it did change, and that is the point of Yeats's poem. It changed horribly. Home Rule passed in the British Parliament, but was set aside at the outbreak of World War I. Irish republicans chose violence as a means to liberation, some of them landing guns from Germany, which was eager to open a second front against the British. Ireland is a small country. Yeats knew many of the men and women organizing for a fight. One of them, Major John MacBride, married the woman Yeats had loved since his twenties, Maud Gonne, who was herself a powerful rabble-rouser willing to suffer for the cause.

Units of the republican army attacked in Dublin during Easter week, 1916. They expected their rebellion to catch fire in the rest of the country, but it did not. Augustine Birrell, Chief Secretary for Ireland, a literary man whose friends included J. M. Barrie, author of *Peter Pan*, reluctantly approved a strong military response. A week of furious battle ended with a siege in the General Post Office on Sackville Street. The city was gutted by artillery, and the last rebels finally surrendered. Friends of Yeats, including Constance Gore-Booth, were imprisoned, while the sixteen leaders of the rebellion, John MacBride among them, were executed by firing squad in the yard of Kilmainham Gaol. It was the start of something. It would lead to the Black and Tans War, the Treaty and Civil War, the Irish Free State and a divided island, and eventually the Republic and the border with Ulster, frustrating England's Brexiters to this day.

The men and women who staged the rebellion were far from ordinary, but the fervor and fanaticism necessary to commit violence of that sort had hardened their purpose. Yeats begins the poem with his own incredulity:

> I have met them at close of day
> Coming with vivid faces
> From counter or desk among grey
> Eighteenth-century houses.

I have passed with a nod of the head
Or polite meaningless words,
Or have lingered a while and said
Polite meaningless words,
And thought before I had done
Of a mocking tale or a gibe
To please a companion
Around the fire at the club,
Being certain that they and I
But lived where motley is worn:
All changed, changed utterly:
A terrible beauty is born.

By then in his fifties, Yeats had perfected a supple technique capable of moving from a bland complacency to extraordinary heights. Here we have his own self-mocking mockery of others—their clownish motley, his jokes at the club. And we arrive at the essence of lyric, the oxymoron in which two words embody irreducible stresses and oppositions, "A terrible beauty"—now the most famous oxymoron in English. In the second stanza he talks of these friends and acquaintances in particular, including Constance Gore-Booth, Padraig Pearse, Thomas MacDonagh, and John MacBride:

That woman's days were spent
In ignorant good-will,
Her nights in argument
Until her voice grew shrill.
What voice more sweet than hers
When, young and beautiful,
She rode to harriers?
This man had kept a school
And rode our wingèd horse;
This other his helper and friend
Was coming into his force;

He might have won fame in the end,
So sensitive his nature seemed,
So daring and sweet his thought.
This other man I had dreamed
A drunken, vainglorious lout.
He had done most bitter wrong
To some who are near my heart,
Yet I number him in the song;
He, too, has resigned his part
In the casual comedy;
He, too, has been changed in his turn,
Transformed utterly:
A terrible beauty is born.

This is the point at which Yeats sees the rebels as individuals, not as symbols or objects of contempt or casual humor. He has not yet named James Connolly, the labor leader who was so badly wounded in battle that he had to be strapped to a chair in order to be executed by the firing squad.

The verse so far is simply articulate, mixing four and three-beat lines, full rhymes with slant surprises like "comedy" and "utterly." A stanza break for Yeats is an opportunity for a change of direction, and he now takes the most surprising turn in the poem. From a tight focus on the particular rebels, he steps back, seeing the whole scene from a distance, as if all human endeavor were no different than the movement of water and the hungers of animals in the wild. The living does not stop with the deaths of particular people. Notice how his focus changes, his attention and alertness becoming almost cinematic:

Hearts with one purpose alone
Through summer and winter seem
Enchanted to a stone
To trouble the living stream.

The horse that comes from the road,
The rider, the birds that range
From cloud to tumbling cloud,
Minute by minute they change;
A shadow of cloud on the stream
Changes minute by minute;
A horse-hoof slides on the brim,
And a horse plashes within it;
The long-legged moor-hens dive,
And hens to moor-cocks call;
Minute by minute they live:
The stone's in the midst of it all.

What is change and what is the unchanging? What is fanaticism? What is the hate that would make people kill each other for some notion of justice? Who is a terrorist and who is a hero in such a context? Yeats, who would later write, "Homer is my example and his unchristened heart," understood a Greek vision of human tragedy, and also understood that violence, like the sex drive, will not simply be wished away, any more than hurricanes and bushfires can be wished away. To seek civility in such a context might be the most powerful thing of all, because it acknowledges the immensity of nature, even of that realm of experience touched by religion.

He asks us to hold this complexity and contradiction in one moment, one oxymoron. What is the beauty, what is the terror of this political and more-than-political moment? And what is the poet to do in the face of such stunning action? Notice how he catches himself in the act of symbolizing, he stops his line of thinking and refuses to let it all be turned into an abstraction:

Too long a sacrifice
Can make a stone of the heart.
O when may it suffice?
That is Heaven's part, our part

To murmur name upon name
As a mother names her child
When sleep at last has come
On limbs that had run wild.
What is it but nightfall?
No, no, not night but death;
Was it needless death after all?
For England may keep faith
For all that is done and said.
We know their dream; enough
To know they dreamed and are dead;
And what if excess of love
Bewildered them till they died?
I write it out in a verse—
MacDonagh and MacBride
And Connolly and Pearse
Now and in time to be,
Wherever green is worn,
Are changed, changed utterly:
A terrible beauty is born.

The green is Ireland, of course, but also a nature that seems certain to outlive all human memory. The poem is not a clarion call to violence, but acknowledges the severity and truth in what these men have done, even if it proves futile.

Yeats has looked at particular people taking an action with which he disagreed, and he has changed his mind about them. He has created a poem that maps the action of his mind, suggesting even a world-mind, a flowing and changing nature of which we are only a part. You can find a work called *The Book of Yeats's Poems*, by the critic Hazard Adams, here in this library, along with maps where I once tried to locate that Belfast park in which I spent the night, maps where you can also find Kastania high in the Greek mountains. In the map room there is even a globe naming all the metaphorical seas of the moon. You can find magazines and journals where new-minted poems appear, novels, memoirs, histories. Yeats's voice is one in a million, one in more than a million to trouble the living stream. What you must cherish if you come to the library is the difficult thing, the effort to tell stories and to listen to them, to slow the urge to judgment, to see.

2020

The Minefield and the Soul

NOTES ON IDENTITY
AND LITERATURE

The purpose of poetry is to remind us
how difficult it is to remain just one person,
for our house is open, there are no keys to the doors,
and invisible guests come in and out at will.

> —Czesław Miłosz

When I was a child I saw
a burning bird in a tree.
I see became I am,
I am became I see.

> —Judith Wright

I identify as *tired.*

> —Hannah Gadsby

What does it mean to see and be seen? These days we make a lot of noise about identity and "identity politics." From some perspectives, it's a misguided tide of righteousness that has destroyed our ability to see each other as individuals, leaving us instead as adherents of groups with greater or lesser moral capital. From others, it's a fundamental cry for justice in a world that has clubbed us with smug assumptions about value and hierarchy for far too long. Anything anyone says is bound to be complicated, contradicted, or made irrelevant by rapidly changing events in the news. My epigraphs above quote two great poets and a comedian, and it may well be that the comedian has spoken more eloquently about identity issues in our time than the poets.

In her powerful Netflix special, *Nanette*, Hannah Gadsby steps boldly into the minefield and exposes it for the complex problem it really is. Anybody and anything can explode at any time. She begins by making fun of the limits of group identity. Already self-identified as gay, she laughs at the criticism she receives from "my people," for somehow not representing group identity properly. It's rather like what Jewish writers like Philip Roth experienced when taken to be spokesmen for a people rather than individuals. Gadsby laughs at those who have told her to come out as transgender, when she doesn't identify that way at all. By the time she says "I identify as *tired*," the laughter releases a huge wave of relief from all quarters. It's something we can share from virtually any point of view. We can identify with her.

But the climax of Gadsby's remarkable monologue exposes another problem of identity. Identity is not merely the possession of an individual saying, "I identify as. . . ." Identity is also the way others see us. These others might be not only our family and friends, with whom we sometimes differ, or the institutions where we work and interact with others, but also truly malevolent people, like the man who beat the shit out of Gadsby simply because of the way he identified her. He hated gay people. He thought beating the shit out of people he considered different was the way a man should behave. The violence and abuse so many have suffered for so long because of their identity—whether defined by race, gender, sexuality, or something else—is what makes any discussion of identity in society, as well as in the arts, particularly fraught.

Aggressions can be subtle. Nearly thirty years ago, I invited an African American novelist to a university where I was teaching, and when I handed him the check for his honorarium he asked me to drive him to a bank where he could deposit it. This was in Minnesota, I should add, a state I once thought enlightened. Too many recent events—shootings, suffocations, etc.—have caused me to feel there is no state in America that is enlightened. The whole country, like the rest of the world, remains in the grip of ancient, intensely ugly animosities. As I parked the car, my friend prepared to enter the bank, turning to me, his hand on the car door, and said, "Here come the fish-eyes."

This was an identifying moment. As a white male, I have never in my life had anyone stare at me oddly or with mistrust when I entered a bank. My friend, a prominent writer and professor, much more successful in the profession than I, had known such experiences all his life. His very name identified him as the descendent of slaves. His prominence as a writer was bound up in the problems of identity.

Others identify us, and I don't imagine many of us are comfortable with that fact. Think of Prufrock:

And I have known the eyes already, known them all—
The eyes that fix you in a formulated phrase,
And when I am formulated, sprawling on a pin,
When I am pinned and wriggling on the wall,
Then how should I begin
To spit out all the butt-ends of my days and ways?
        And how should I presume?

Most of us like to think we can own our own identity, and that's one of the problems of the minefield. We can't own our *selves*. We don't really own anything.

YET SOME FORM of autonomy is essential for our very survival, our ability to stand up and walk into a room and function. Some form of individual dignity and respect for the dignity of others remains an essential human value. This value is in terrible jeopardy in our time, when even empathy, the ability to identify with others, is under attack on both the Left and the Right. On the Left we often have writers saying they own their experience and no one else has the right to imagine experiences like theirs. On the Right we find the experiences of others denied by a whitewashing of history and a pretense that values we correlate with civilization have never been compromised by racism or other primitive ideologies. But the experience of a character is not your experience or my experience. It is the experience of *that character*. Literature invites us into a third dimension where we might meet in our effort to understand not just ourselves but others. Really *others*. As often as not, literature shows us people in conflict with the very notion of identity. If we insist that it conform to any particular code of values or identities, we miss the opportunity to have our experience complicated and enriched.

When I say identity is an illusion, I have no intention of denying your reality and autonomy. That, as one of Prufrock's confronters said, is "not what I meant at all." I do not mean to deny individuality the way a corporate or state bureaucracy denies individuality in order to subjugate it, regulate it, or rob us of value. I mean instead to augment the idea of self by suggesting it may be permeable and multiple and ultimately unknowable. Respect for the dignity of others comes partly from an acknowledgment that we are equal in the fact of our suffering, no matter what the degree and variety of our suffering may have been.

That's the ideal, anyway. It is not always possible to respect others as one would wish. Dictators and white supremacists come to mind. The late V. S. Naipaul had, like Joseph Conrad, a sort of jaundiced fascination with and revulsion to some truly horrible figures. Naipaul's occasional misanthropy has, since his death in 2018, been the subject of renewed debate and controversy. But one doesn't have to agree with his vision in order to read his novels.

This is where the poets I quote in my epigraphs come in handy. Literature involves us in the mystery of identity because it is made by individuals who often find identity problematic. Czesław Miłosz, the Polish Nobel laureate, had felt the pressures of war and dictatorship, and reminds us of the many unlocked doors, like miraculously opened prison cells, in the imagination. It is indeed hard "to remain just one person"— and why would one want to? Perhaps he thought of the Roman playwright Terence, who said, "I am human. Nothing human is alien to me." Or perhaps he recalled Keats, whose letter to Richard Woodhouse (October 27, 1818) remains one of the great statements of poetics:

> As to the poetical Character itself (I mean that sort of which, if I am any thing, I am a Member; that sort distinguished from the wordsworthian or egotistical sublime; which is a thing per se and stands alone) it is not itself—it has no self—it is everything thing and nothing—It has no character—it enjoys light and shade; it lives in gusto, be it foul or fair, high or low, rich or poor, mean or elevated—it has as much delight in conceiving an Iago as an Imogen. What shocks the virtuous philosopher, delights the camelion Poet. . . . A Poet is the most unpoetical of any thing in existence; because he has no Identity—he is continually in for—and filling some other Body— The Sun, the Moon, the Sea and Men and Women who are creatures of impulse and are poetical and have about them an unchangeable attribute—the poet has none; no identity—he is certainly the most unpoetical of all God's Creatures.

Maybe I love this letter because I feel "camelion" myself. (I'm also a terrible speller.) Keats pits the free imagination against a sort of puritanical virtue. Writers wishing to be socially or politically virtuous can lose their interest in artful ambiguity, becoming absolutist in their judgments. In his letter, Keats toys with our attachment to identity. He concludes as follows:

> But even now I am perhaps not speaking from myself: but from some character in whose soul I now live. I am sure however that this next sentence is from myself. I feel your anxiety, good opinion and friendliness in the highest degree, and am
>
> Yours most sincerely,
John Keats

He signs his *name*—not "Nobody," not "Nemo." Does one write poetry to have a name, an identity, fame? Or does one write and read to have *more life*—including more diversity of life, more identities? Surely both motives can be true.

My second epigraph, from Australian poet Judith Wright, makes poetic being and poetic seeing understandable in human terms. Writers have no special dispensation for anything in this world, but our lives are smaller, our vision more pedestrian without the words they offer us. They make contingent meanings beautiful. Judith Wright's poetry is full of superb observations of nature, particularly of birds—the best poets often have a bit of the scientist in them. Wright gives me more diversity of life by writing as accurately as she does. I don't come to literature for affirmation of my own experience, but to be awakened and involved more fully in life, including the lives of others.

I AM MOST INTRIGUED by writing that eludes the sort of easy definition a journalist contrives to pitch a story to an editor. Imagine pitching *Hamlet* or *Ulysses* or *Their Eyes Were Watching God* to an impresario who needs it nailed in two sentences. "Middle-aged Jewish cuckold wanders Dublin trying to place an ad. Meets young, insufferable, and soused writer and takes him home for creaturely cocoa." It doesn't work. But *Ulysses* does. How would Zora Neale Hurston's novel be pitched? "A light-skinned Black woman, descended from two generations of rape, tells of her growing up and three marriages. One of her marriages ends in murder." The pitch conveys nothing of Hurston's gorgeous prose or the way she complicates both race and gender.

The writing I love eludes paraphrase, exhausts criticism, and complicates experience—as true of Mother Goose as of James Joyce. It rewards re-reading, outflanks marketing categories, and sometimes even transcends our assertions that writers should represent a gender or race or class. I am aware of my privilege as a straight white male. Sometimes I even apologize for it. But I have also been young, old, foreign, married, divorced, unemployed, and deaf. I have been a fisherman and cannery worker, gardener, teacher, and a state laureate. I've never felt that I was living as if identity didn't matter. I argue that identity, for an artist, is not *one thing*—and I suspect this is true for most individuals, despite our human tendency to judge by appearances. For an artist, one ennobling ambition is to empathize with multiple identities. At times I have played a middle-aged woman, or a gay shopkeeper, or a part Cherokee dealer in artifacts, or a Greek immigrant, or a girl whose parents were Mexican and Welsh—all characters I have explored in verse. Doing so did not appropriate anyone else's experience, but created another experience altogether. There is a realm of make-believe where identity cannot be entirely fixed, and we enlarge experience there. Literature asks us to open ourselves to more fluid states of being that actually reflect our reality. It honors doubt and ambiguity and multiple points of view.

It's not that I believe in one standard thing you can call "literary." I couldn't begin to pitch my definition, except to say that literature is the kind of writing it is hard to kill or to forget, and even that is obviously insufficient. I read to be changed. To be moved. This is the beginning of compassion for others.

We are all so much more, and so much less, than our social and psychic identity. Even biology—our interconnected DNA—demonstrates both individuality and interrelatedness.

Literature allows us to see this as an opportunity for getting through or beyond the single ego. I have always argued for the legitimacy of any literary technique—the viability of so-called free verse, for example, as well as rhyme and meter. But I continually meet people, including poets, who misunderstand the freedom of the verbal arts, assuming that constraints such as rhyme prevent us from saying what we "really mean." Yes, I answer, and thank God they do. What we *mean*, what we *intend*, locks us into an egocentric room; it's a poor substitute for the multiple windows offered by language itself, or other surprising sources of inspiration. The late Geoffrey Hill put it this way in a *Paris Review* interview:

> A great deal of the work of the last forty years seems to me to spring from inadequate knowledge and self-knowledge, a naïve trust in the unchallengeable authority of the authentic self.... There is a kind of poetry—I think that the seventeenth-century English metaphysicals are the greatest examples of this, Donne, Herbert, Vaughan—in which the language seems able to hover above itself in a kind of brooding, contemplative, self-rectifying way. It is probably true of the very greatest writers. I think it's true of Dante and Milton, and I think it's true of Wordsworth.... The rest of us, even the very best of us, possess it to a lesser and differing degree, but I cannot conceive poetry of any enduring significance being brought into being without some sense of this double quality that language has when it is taken into the sensuous intelligence, and brought into formal life.

The "sensuous intelligence" cannot be given a simple name. I have never felt I had a single voice. Call it a limitation—call it unmarketable—but it's what I really feel. Sometimes it's religion showing up where least expected—a sort of Buddhist realization that the self is an illusion. Mostly it's just awareness of the psyche's permeability and a strange joy in not dragging a leaden *Dave* around all day. I read and write for dilation, which is its own pleasure.

In literature, meaning is rarely one thing; instead it is a field of possibilities. I'm not saying a poem means anything you want it to, but if it's a good poem the meanings multiply, the readings like half-hidden animal tracks in the woods. Poetry has the heart of an anarchist. It celebrates prestidigitation and has something in common with the clown and the stand-up comedian. The imagination is free.

AND FREEDOM CAN be scary. In 1941, a time of acute pressure on all things earthly, with real minefields proliferating nearly everywhere, the psychologist Erich Fromm published *Escape from Freedom*. His preface posits "the full realization of positive freedom which is based upon the uniqueness and individuality of man." Fromm's definition must have seemed particularly urgent in a time of vast armies, global disaster. Many of those who felt "a horror of aloneness" sought to relinquish freedom to the will of an authoritarian leader of one kind or another. The fight against totalitarian systems required a belief in the free and independent individual. But Fromm also understood that political freedom does not free us. In order to live in open societies, we must understand our own fragility and that of others. We must be willing to risk the perhaps meaningless silence underlying our existence.

To the creative spirit, some ability to live with uncertainty is a prerequisite. Writing to his brothers in December 1817, Keats said it in these now famous words:

I had not a dispute but a disquisition with Dilke, upon various subjects; several things dove-tailed in my mind, and at once it struck me what quality went to form a Man of Achievement, especially in literature, and which Shakespeare possessed so enormously—I mean Negative Capability, that is, when a man is capable of being in uncertainties, mysteries, doubts, without any irritable reaching after fact and reason. . . .

His idea is worth considering for the experience it makes available to us. That "irritable reaching after fact and reason" is not Keats's rejection of Apollonian thinking, but his awareness of its blockages, its borders. Our best writers do seem to cultivate this "negative capability." Think of novelists like Virginia Woolf and Willa Cather who wrote equally well about both men and women, peace and war. When Keats in a later letter called the world "a vale of soul-making," he expressed the defiant faith of an artist, a maker.

Miguel de Unamuno had something like this in mind when he wrote about the limits of identity in *The Tragic Sense of Life*:

> . . . nothing is the same for two successive moments of its being. My idea of God is different each time I conceive it. Identity, which is death, is precisely what the intellect seeks. The mind seeks what is dead, for the living escapes it. It seeks to congeal the flowing stream into blocks of ice. It seeks to arrest the flow.

I don't mean to disparage the intellect here, only to suggest that our certainties are often not worth holding.

Yet there are certainly circumstances when one's nationality and other forms of identity become undeniable. The world can very cruelly make it so. Someone may shoot you for the color of your skin or enclose you in barbed wire. Bullies and brutes may beat you for whatever they think you are. People may be derided or ignored unjustly. These things are only too real, and we must resist them in any way we can. Literature is part of that resistance, not because it teaches us some monolithic virtue, but by helping us navigate the complex and contradictory realities of life, helping us feel the realities of others. Ultimately, literature declares its liberty even when it sings in its chains like the sea. Writers know they are all leading posthumous existences, communing with the dead in their separate, solitary ways, and that nothing, not even language, saves any of us. Except when it *does*.

2019

Poet and Moralist

CLAUDIA RANKINE AND KAY RYAN

Join me down here in nowhere.
—Claudia Rankine

      No
loss is token.
—Kay Ryan

THE BEST WRITING trusts readers to find their own way through its thickets, challenging them along the way. But it also leaves us with memorable language, something we can carry through to our lives, and in that way it is *helpful*. Both writers considered here, Claudia Rankine and Kay Ryan, are highly regarded for their work, both are called poets, though one seems to have invented her own extra-literary discourse while the other, equally serious, comes across with transcendent delight. A comparison of these two very different approaches might prove instructive. If literature can change us, it seems not to be in a way that satisfies our desire for immediate and lasting social justice. It is not just in our politics that literature affects change, but in our mode of being.

Claudia Rankine's *Citizen* is a devastating book—one every American should read. Is it poetry? I don't know, though the question is important. Provocatively subtitled "An American Lyric," the book is much more than conceptual art—genre-bending at the very least. The helpless feeling it produces about how we read and misread each other might be called lyrical, but Rankine's methods are deliberately anti-poetic. You could call it creative nonfiction with mixtures of journalism, anecdotal prose, verse, and collage (including visual art that has to be read as carefully as the language). Whatever you call it, *Citizen* is an education in the micro- and macroaggressions that so often define American race relations. It seems to me that, no matter where we stand on Rankine's work as poetry, we cannot deny its relevance to social justice, and we might as well start there, with the admission that social justice is important, though it can easily compromise that other realm of experience, the universal intensity we find in the best poetry.

Like many other books on the topics of race and gender, *Citizen* is fundamentally existential. We usually understand identity in social terms—one is labeled by others, or one identifies with a group. Race and gender appear to make these group identities ineluctable, even if no individual feels fully identified by such terms. Yet even one's race and gender can be misread or misused in our assumptions. The self can be far more fleeting or illusory than identity politics allow.

Rankine explores multiple sides of these dilemmas. In a central essay, the example and metaphor of tennis allows her to discuss not only the genius of Serena Williams but also ways in which the tennis great is judged as a Black woman—skin color, body type, gender, fashion, and language all have bearing on the case. Tennis is, like art, a field of play in which social assumptions and interactions are illuminated. Like literature, it has had a certain clubbiness in its history, and the game is enriched when that exclusivity begins to dissolve. In a later prose anecdote, Rankine, who has won many prizes for her work and has taught at elite universities, returns from a tennis game of her own and is asked if she won. "It wasn't a match," she says. "It was a lesson." Her book is essentially didactic, and that is precisely why it does not entirely win me over. The book's rhetoric assumes an unthinking readership who have to be taught. For example, she reprints a famous photograph of a lynching, but erases the Black bodies hanging from a tree because she assumes we would only focus on them and not the faces of the ordinary Americans who have gathered to watch the killing like spectators at a carnival. But how can she assume she knows how each of us might read that photo? Her technique implies a mistrust of the viewer and reader.

Claudia Rankine does not need to control the reading to such a degree. Simple observation is enough to indict the layers of self-deception, falsehood, misreading, and outright hate found in our social relations. She quotes filmmaker Claire Denis: "I don't want to be a nurse or a doctor, I just want to be an observer." But Rankine offers her observations in a relentless second-person voice, making readers identify as protagonists: "When you are alone and too tired even to turn on any of your devices, you let yourself linger in a past stacked among your pillows." There is more indictment here, and the author does not present herself as being above such defenses as "devices" and comforting pillows, or a voice telling her as a child, "You smell good." There's an exhausted, hollowed-out grief running through the book. "Tried rhyme," she writes, "tried truth, tried epistolary untruth, tried and tried." It all feels more urgent in a time when Americans shoot first and ask questions later. A Katrina montage comprising quotes from CNN and another called "Stop-and-Frisk" expose more of the macroaggressions Black people in America continually face.

The situation is dire, and the culture's violence—"America turned loose on America"—would seem to preclude any possibility of leavening humor. There's little or no comedy in *Citizen*, though for one brief moment there is laughter:

> When the waitress hands your friend the card she took from you, you laugh and ask what else her privilege gets her? Oh, my perfect life, she answers. Then you both are laughing so hard, everyone in the restaurant smiles.

Rankine's deliberate ambiguity with pronouns often prevents us from knowing precisely who is talking and who is being addressed. What about issues of class and money in this short excerpt? Who is judge? Who is judged? Rankine's observations apply to all such questions, and to the solitary person navigating perilous waters.

Citizen is artful, open to complex readings, but must we call it poetry? Perhaps only if we want to tear down genre definitions and glorify our independence in the process. Quite aside from such ambitions, language can give us different kinds of experience, even political experience, that we call poetic and that have to do with particularly charged and "musical" textures. When, in her brief verse section, Rankine writes, "The patience is in the living. Time opens out to you," I could be hearing the T. S. Eliot of "Four Quartets." This makes me wonder what would happen if a writer of Rankine's fierce magnitude returned more fully to verse and trusted her readers more. But, of course, her work then would have far less social impact. Rankine is the artist as moralist, and may have given up on poetry's ambiguity and grace for a more direct and prosecutorial stance. Patience indeed.

IN THE REMARKABLE POETRY of Kay Ryan, on the other hand, issues of self and identification seem entirely absent, or are treated with bemused skepticism. Rankine tells stories about human erasure, while Ryan creates playful but resounding riddles:

Erasure

We just don't
know what
erases what
or much about
the deep nature
of erasure. But
these places with
rubbery crumbs
are exciting us
currently; this
whole area
may have been
a defactory.

There is defacement in that last astonishing word, and the poem exists not only at the social level but also the cosmic one. Ryan can wring wryness even out of her griefs. "Death has a life / of its own," she writes, making characteristically subtle use of the line break. Her brief, innovative lyrics upend consensus by challenging us to complete them. They have the audacious generosity to treat us as equals.

Having served two terms as U.S. Poet Laureate and won the Pulitzer Prize for her wittily-titled selected poems, *The Best of It*, Ryan has a reputation for comedy—and she is as funny as they come—but her poems are often tough-minded deconstructions of language and experience, exposing a grief within and between words. A poem from her "selected" called "The Excluded Animals" manages to bring up microaggressions in human judgments while delighting in the sounds our mouths can make: "Only a certain / claque of beasts / is part of the / crèche racket." She celebrates the verse culture of rhyme, while her social observations, though angular, are as acute as anyone's.

Her recent collection, *Erratic Facts*, is recognizably Ryan—still refusing to hew to any self-identification, still using rhymed free verse, still playfully cracking open common phrases and arcane knowledge. The erratics of her title are boulders left behind by glaciers, but she's not preaching global warming to us. She's talking, among many other things, about forces beyond our individual lives, the aspect of geological time and the chilling experience of a lover's death.

Eggs

We turn out
as tippy as
eggs. Legs
are an illusion.
We are held
as in a carton
if someone
loves us.
It's a pity
only loss
proves this.

Everything is indirection—a trait she shares with Emily Dickinson, to whom she is compared so often it must drive her nuts. In these new poems we become aware that something has changed:

New Rooms

The mind must
set itself up
wherever it goes
and it would be
most convenient
to impose its

old rooms—just
take them up
like an interior
tent. Oh but
the new holes
aren't where
the windows
went.

It's a set-up, all right, this life and death. And dealing with it, the mind sets *itself* up. We find ourselves in a looking-glass world of half-familiar, half-estranging architecture, and in grief we cannot see to see. Ryan's long-time partner, Carol Adair, died in 2009, and the most devastating line in this book is its dedication: "for Carol anyhow."

The uncanniness of Ryan's poetry lies in her ability to convey these common griefs while allowing us simultaneously to delight in her art. She refuses sentimentality, refuses to personalize, gives us pleasure while compelling us to re-read. Having our minds changed by new insight is affirming in itself. The way she trusts us to get it, meets us halfway in the spaces between her whimsical lines, gives her poems an alchemical quality I rarely find in contemporary poetry. I'm sure Rankine, too, would recognize the use of the word "citizen" in Ryan's "The Obsoletion of Language":

We knew it
would happen,
one of the laws.
And that it
would be this
sudden: words
become a chewing
action of the jaws
and mouth, unheard

by the only other
citizen there was
on earth.

We can talk about all the social things here, and the recognition of equality in another person, but when language becomes a meaningless jawing we find ourselves alone on a barren heath, a place of existential terror and psychic survival. Ryan would never pretend to such big ideas, but I'm finding them all over her work, which is poetry of the highest order.

I find Ryan's work more satisfying as *literature*, which demands that I examine my terms. Clearly, literature can be concerned with social justice—we see this in works from Shakespeare's *Othello* to Dickens's *Oliver Twist*, Steinbeck's *The Grapes of Wrath* and Toni Morrison's *Beloved*. But in none of these works I call literary is the writer primarily a preacher telling me what I need to learn and how I ought to feel about it. The writer instead compels an understanding of human complexity, mixed emotions, ambiguity, and is concerned with saying things in a luminous as well as an illuminating way.

One danger we face as a society is the way our demands for social justice might drown out voices of ambiguity and complexity. Real literature, it seems to me, will always resist this flattening of human experience, this way of conforming to political causes. Real literature trusts us to act politically in the political realm, and to develop our understanding of life on earth by all imaginative means available to us. It may be a messy profession, but it is not without honor.

2016

Daughters of Memory

THE SIBLING RIVALRY
OF HISTORY AND POETRY

1. The Motive for Story

History and poetry grew up in the same family, but what a strange, dysfunctional brood they have become in our era of academic specialization, when every pursuit becomes a "field," weeded and watched over by professionals. Our claims for authority appear to be very different from those of Homer or Herodotus. Yet while the means of publication and the available evidence for our stories have changed, I doubt we are more sophisticated than the ancients. It helps to remember the Muses as Hesiod met them on Mt. Helicon—all nine of them daughters of Memory, or Mnemosyne:

> And when the time came, as the months passed away and the seasons turned about, and the long table of days was completed, she bore nine daughters—all of one mind, their carefree hearts set on song—not far from the topmost peak of snowy Olympus. There they have their dancing-places and

their mansions; and the Graces and Desire dwell beside them, in feasting. Lovely is the sound they produce from their mouths as they sing and celebrate the ordinances and the good ways of all the immortals, making delightful utterance. (M. L. West translation)

Clio, the muse of history, makes "delightful utterance" as much as Calliope or Erato, epic or lyric poetry, and all three are the sisters of music and dance. The story is instructive. We moderns have too often insisted on separating the sisters. We become Gradgrinds, clinging to our facts, when we might remember that stories can sing. I am not talking about the factless universe of Donald Trump here, or "fake news" in all its variants, but a way of living in relation to the truth without absolute knowledge, a humane coexistence with uncertainty and doubt.

If histories can strive to make harmonious sounds, poems can remember historical events. We harvest the same field—memory—after all. We think of the epic as a poem of history, though here, as in Herodotus, history and mythology are hard to tell apart. Ezra Pound thought of his *Cantos* as a vast synthesis of historical themes, while Robert Lowell wrote sequences of sonnets on history. Both of these modern poets left more muddle than they had hoped. "History has to live with what was here," Lowell wrote, "clutching and close to fumbling all we had. . . ." His poems make diverting reading as adjuncts to autobiography, but wouldn't satisfy anyone seeking more general information.

My own effort to write an epic, a modern historical poem, deliberately mixes fact and fiction, as did Shakespeare in his history plays, or Tolstoy in *War and Peace*. I called *Ludlow* a verse novel, a more modest-sounding term than epic, but more than a decade after the book was first published I can see how oddly it sits in terms of genre. My motives and methods for this story differ from those of an historian. I want to make experience immersive and present, even as I probe the motives of all involved. The historian, like the good journalist, wishes to establish facts, while the poet might say, as I do in *Ludlow*, "These are the facts, but facts are not the story."*

These are thorny distinctions, pricking away at our absolute confidence, which is why it remains helpful to remember Hesiod and the family of Muses. In his *Poetics*, Aristotle tried to give the disciplines their separate roles:

> It will be clear from what I have said that it is not the poet's function to describe what has actually happened, but the kind of thing that might happen, that is, that could happen because they are, in the circumstances, either probable or necessary. The difference between the historian and the poet is not that one writes in prose and the other in verse; the work of Herodotus might be put into verse, and in this material form it would be no less a kind of history than it is without metre. The difference is that one tells of what has happened, the other of the kinds of things that might happen. For this reason poetry is something more philosophical and more worthy of serious attention than history; for poetry speaks more of universals, history of particulars. (Penelope Murray and T. S. Dorsch translation)

Aristotle's genre distinctions don't quite do the job, at least when we look at particular examples. Sometimes poetry is more interested in particulars, history in universals, and both deserve "serious attention." They also deserve unserious attention for the pleasure they can give us.

Aristotle's desire to place the genres on a hierarchical scale smacks of poetry's origins in religious ritual, with its primordial authority and mystery. The first known epic poem, *Gil-*

---

*I hasten to add that I am not comparing my work to the work of these masters, only saying they inspired me to make the attempt.

gamesh, was inscribed on tablets and buried in the city walls, as if the poem, which was also a story, were the very foundation of civic life:

> The Story
> of him who knew the most of all men know;
> who made the journey; heartbroken; reconciled;
>
> who knew the way things were before the Flood,
> the secret things, the mystery; who went
>
> to the end of the earth, and over; who returned,
> and wrote the story on a tablet of stone.
>
> He built Uruk. He built the keeping place
> of Anu and Ishtar. The outer wall
>
> shines in the sun like brightest copper; the inner
> wall is beyond the imagining of kings.
>
> (David Ferry translation)

Talk about unspecialized! Gilgamesh is both hero and poet here, and also the king and builder of the city. The story is enshrined in all its ambiguity. We might well ask ourselves what modern stories could be planted in American foundations. What is the making and the make-up of Americans? What is this experiment in personhood, so vital and so precarious? Surely there cannot be only one epic of the United (or the disunited) States. There would have to be many, and perhaps my own "long poem" will be among them.

2. Ludlow, *Poetry and History*

The event now known as the Ludlow Massacre took place on April 20, 1914, in the southern Colorado coal fields. Immigrants from more than twenty countries mined coal in brutal conditions at a time when anti-immigrant feeling was very high. The United Mine Workers union sought to gain a foot-hold among these workers and infiltrated their ranks, argu-ing for an eight-hour day, safer conditions, and legal tender for pay rather than company scrip. On the other side, the company hired private detectives and other thugs to keep order. A strike was declared in the fall of 1913. Things quickly went from terri-ble to worse, with beatings and killings on both sides, until the Governor called in the National Guard to keep order. Unfortu-nately, order was not kept. The union organized strikers in tent camps and brought in rabble-rousing speakers like Mother Jones. The soldiers' ranks contained veterans of wars in Mex-ico and the Philippines, and racism inflamed their anti-immi-grant anger. When the State of Colorado could no longer afford to pay the soldiers' salaries, the company took over the payroll. The troops could see what side their bread was buttered on.

If Shakespeare's Hotspur, to use another figure recreated in historical verse, is motivated partly by hate, so were both sides in the Ludlow conflict. The force of the irrational runs through history and literature because it runs through human-ity, and while history may seek to understand its causes, liter-ature tends to be more fatalistic about human nature. Acts of kindness and generosity mean so much to us partly because of the bitter contexts in which they occur. We have competing narratives about what happened on April 20, 1914—the union side and the company side. Who opened fire first? Who was responsible for the conflict? At the end of the day, more than twenty people were dead—even this number is disputed and uncertain. Thirteen of them were women and children who suffocated in a pit under one of the strikers' tents. The tents had been set aflame and the whole camp at Ludlow burned. The photographic evidence of catastrophic fire is indisputable, but precisely who set the tents alight remains a subject of con-troversy. My own strong feeling is that the soldiers burned the camp, not knowing there were people hiding under the tents. They had attacked the camps on previous occasions, and this was part of their strategy, a prelude to scorched earth tactics in our many wars.

One of the best histories of the Ludlow Massacre was written by journalist Scott Martelle, whose years working as a reporter for the *Los Angeles Times* and other newspapers trained him in research. He agrees about the basic facts I have outlined above, and suggests that "Massacre" is the wrong word for what transpired, because it implies that the soldiers deliberately set out to kill women and children that day. He would call it a battle instead, perhaps one involving that despicable term "collateral damage." I have heard Martelle patiently make this case in rooms full of people still seething with outrage and unable to hear him. Ludlow was a terrible event, and has been used by both sides for propaganda. Talking about Ludlow in the nearby town of Trinidad, where my own father was born and raised, can get you into trouble. If this is history, it is so close to us that the wounds still fester.

I had heard about Ludlow from my father and his brothers, rather like Herodotus hearing from the Delphians. I had read *The Great Coalfield War* (1996), by George S. McGovern and Leonard F. Guttridge, and I had grown up among left-leaning people in Washington State, prone to sympathize with striking immigrants. The election of 2000, decided by a Supreme Court vote, had outraged me to the point where I questioned the legitimacy of the Bush presidency. I questioned it further when my country invaded Iraq, a country with a terrible regime, to be sure, but one that had not attacked us in the first place. I was angry about American politics, about ways in which corporate power seemed rampant and anti-immigrant feeling was again on the rise. I was also married to a Scottish immigrant and had spent much of my life among Greek immigrants. When I read *Buried Unsung: Louis Tikas and the Ludlow Massacre* (1991), by Zeese Papanikolas, I began to feel I had ways of approaching the story that made my attempt inevitable.

Tikas, whose real name was Ilias Spantidakis, was from

Crete. He became a union organizer and was shot in the back by militia troops on the day of the massacre, a Monday following the Orthodox Easter Sunday. I had lived in Greece and spoke the language. After twenty years of wandering, I had recently moved back to Colorado, where I had family roots and felt I knew the land and the people well enough to write about them. I had also written narrative and dramatic poetry for much of my life, and wanted to expand my technical range and call upon earlier efforts to write fiction at the same time. I was made to write *Ludlow*. The only question was how to do it.

Two things occurred to me right away: first, I would use blank verse, giving myself permission to vary it whenever needed, and I would learn from poets like Derek Walcott about macaronic diction, ways of making the language of a place out of the many languages of its people. Second, I would mix historical figures with fictional ones, trying to make them equally real to each other and to my readers. I would try to get Clio and Calliope to sing together. My main historical character, Louis Tikas, was accessible partly through the research of Papanikolas, partly through my experience of Greek immigrants, the hyphenated identities of Greek-Americans and the textures of Greek village life. My main fictional character, Luisa Mole, her name a sort of mirror of Louis's, grew in many ways from my own psyche, my own feeling of crushed and splintered identity. As I would write in a note to the second edition of the book, "Our nation has since its founding produced a series of experiments into the nature of individuality. What is a person? Who has the right to exist in this place? Fiction asks such questions as urgently as history does."

Something was in the air, because Scott Martelle's *Blood Passion: The Ludlow Massacre and Class Warfare in the American West* came out at almost precisely the same time in 2007 as *Ludlow*. I didn't have the benefit of Scott's insights when I wrote my narrative poem, but we've since become friends, and have been called upon more than once, along with Zeese and others, to discuss the Ludlow Massacre at conferences. We happen to agree on the narrative and its meaning, but all three of us came at it from different directions, often with different motives. In our time, the poet usually comes across in these discussions as the least authoritative figure. People really do want to know the facts, and the historians have done a very good job of demonstrating those facts, yet ambiguities remain in spite of their best efforts. I wanted to dwell with those ambiguities and the shadings of character, as well as to use everything I knew about writing verse.

By now, Ludlow has been the subject of films, books, and articles by many hands, yet my poetic version of the story may have struck its own chord. In 2019, the scholar Yiorgos Anagnostou published an essay called "Poetry Traversing History: Narrating Louis Tikas in David Mason's *Ludlow*," which makes an argument for poetic truth in harmony with history:

> An additional narrative route in *Ludlow*'s evocation of immigrant subjectivity travels through sheer poetic imagination. . . . a thread in the poem explicitly imagines Tikas. It visualizes his most intimate moments, including those that take place in brothels. Or it ventures into picturing Tikas sleepless, yearning for the sensual pleasures of his natal place—the sea, the smells—missing what "was almost freedom." . . . this poetic excavation of private moments brings to life experiences and feelings that largely escape the historical archive. . . . History's turn to subjectivity and *Ludlow*'s respective interest in these "most uncompromising places" [a phrase quoted from Michel Foucault] converge then in valuing precisely the exploration of areas of human experience that are prone to elude the archive.

Could poetry be another form of history?

Ludlow would not work as fiction to the degree it does without my trying to imagine the inner lives of my characters, giving them what I call "ground sense," the feeling of what it might be like to inhabit their skin, their minds. My Tikas might not be the real one, but neither is the historian's. We are both storytellers, after all. I tried to see Tikas as a man who dreams, who suffers, who desires. In the following passage, before his involvement with union politics, he has just begun working in the mines—another activity I had to imagine for myself with no actual experience of it:

Mountains. Distant sea a dream above the olives.
His sisters going out to milk the goats
while he repaired a terrace wall. The weight
of stones.
      He woke with burning hands,
the pain of blisters, in a man-packed room
dark as the chambered pit but full of snores.
The freedom of his dreams
far off as sunlight on a swirling cove.

For all the years he'd lived in America
he'd felt the torture of its emptiness.
the quiet of a village just at nightfall,
goat bells, women's voices, rustle of leaves,
came back as steadily as waves, as wind
in olive branches he had climbed as a boy
to feel them swaying like small boats at sea.
He felt that constant sway and almost cried.

Already Louis knew that he would quit,
but when and how, how many Greeks he'd take
straight to the union hall in Frederick—
those were questions that disturbed his sleep.
How they would leave. How pass the guarded gate.
He'd seen detectives in a motorcar,
armed men from Baldwin-Felts,
the agency well known for breaking strikes.

And so he rose and worked, went down the pit
and learned to push his fear still deeper down.
The men who argued at the scales were beaten
senseless by the guards while Tikas watched,
but each night after work the men would talk
of *apergíes*, strikes, and what it meant
to be a scab, and how long they would wait
and what some unarmed men could do to guards.

Imagining Luisa Mole, the child of a Welsh father and a Mexican mother, was really no different. The material at hand was everything I knew in my skin and nerves and, in a peculiar way, everything I remembered.

I'll finish this discussion with one event, two narrations, the historical and the poetic. Scott Martelle's book opens with a gunfight:

Trinidad, August 16, 1913. Gerald Lippiatt, a stocky man with a bushy mustache, scuffed up little puffs of dust as he walked the slight rise of North Commercial Street between the Purgatoire River and the small buildings marking downtown's outer edge. It was a few minutes after eight o'clock on a Saturday night, and the late summer sun had given way to a full moon that bathed the prairie-edge city in gentle light. A dry easterly breeze slipping in from the Sangre de Cristo Mountains carried away the last vestiges of a hot and dry day. As Lippiatt, an organizer for the United Mine Workers of America, neared the heart of downtown, he was swallowed by the festive energy of people shaking off the exacting drudgery of a week working on the ranch or mining coal deep below the ground. Blue sparks flashed from overhead wires as electric trolleys rumbled along brick-lined tracks, and at the city center, where Commercial Street crossed Main in front of the posh Columbian Hotel, a Salvation Army minister exhorted sinners to repent, his message stopping at the doors of busy first-floor saloons, pawnshops, and narrow gambling halls.

The setting is absolutely convincing. Martelle has done his work, researching and triangulating details to establish his facts, building on his experience of the weather, the photographic evidence, etc. Lippiatt knew he was in trouble before he went to Trinidad. He knew how dangerous it was. No sooner had he arrived on Commercial Street than he fell into an argument with Baldwin-Felts detectives. Guns were drawn. Lippiatt went down in a hail of bullets, wounding one detective in the leg. Those are the events, and they are as factual as anything can be.

My own narration of the gunfight happens from Luisa's point of view. When the shooting starts, she's with the Reed household across the river, caring for their children. Mr. Reed is away, working in his mercantile store in town, close to the intersection of Commercial and Main Streets. By now, we know that Luisa has an unspoken crush on George Reed, and when the shooting starts, her first thought is of him:

After she put Pud down at his bedtime
Luisa sat on the steps to the front porch
to catch the evening breeze.
The girls were playing jump-rope in the yard
and Mrs. Reed, her mending basket out,
rocked and looked at the view of Fisher's Peak.
The men worked late a summer Saturday.
Luisa gazed across at town, the river.

That was where they came from—pistol shots
in quick succession: POP-POP-POP. POP-POP.
A ricochet of sound from buildings where
Commercial Street fanned out above the river.
"What in tarnation?" Mrs. Reed had stood.

POP-POP. POP-POP. POP-POP. Luisa ran
almost before she knew it—wind rushing
past her ears, black hair flying. Behind her

voices screamed. "Luisa, no!" But no one
followed as she crossed the thumping bridge,
more people near, then running too like her,
both men and women. Then they were a crowd
and she stopped running. Motorcars and people
jammed the street outside the union office.
She saw the smashed glass of a shop window,
the bullet holes and chips in the brick walls.

A man lay on the street, holding his knee
and cursing like a soldier. Another man
lay twisted on a thick stream of his blood.
Some women screamed. Policemen cleared a way
to get an ambulance to the wounded man.
Luisa stood, relieved it wasn't George.
No, it was George Reed standing next to her:
"What the hell are you doing here, young lady?"

He'd put his collar on, his coat and tie
with its cigar smells. Sometimes, walking home,
he liked to smoke, and maybe stop to drink
just one with Arthur before he crossed the bridge.
She felt him turn her from the sight and walk
deliberately away, his hand upon
her shoulder, steadying her shaking bones.
"Who was that man?" she asked. "The one who died?"

"Some union fella, came in on the train.
I heard him having words with two mine guards
or detectives or whatever the hell they are."
He stopped and turned her toward him, and she saw
worry in his blue eyes. "It's getting worse,
young lady. More union men arriving

every week, and more detectives. These fellas
argued. I didn't see who started shooting. . . ."

My motives here are multiple. I want to move the action forward and create suspense, to illuminate the psychology of my
characters as best I can. George Reed is a businessman, suspicious of both sides, who simply wants to stay out of trouble,
Luisa a divided soul, conflicted in her loyalties and affections.
Scott Martelle's narrative establishes the facts, while mine
deals with the feelings of my characters. Neither approach
denies the truth of what happened that day, as far as it can
be known.

While my sympathies lie almost entirely with the immigrants, I made sure not to see the union as a choir of angels.
The roughness and brutality of both sides is truer to the facts.
But I also don't want to deny my outrage at the soullessness of
corporations and their henchmen, the incompetence of politi-
cians, the thwarted hopes of all who wished to keep the peace.
I want that complication and ambiguity not only because it
seems truer to the facts as we know them but because it more
accurately represents the complications of life.

Memory is memory, made up of imagination as much as
a kind of cellular truth. According to myth, she is an unreliable mother, a mysterious figure whose nine daughters once
were joined in "delightful utterance." Viewing them as absolutely separate creatures isolates them in a cold universe, dis-
connected from meaning with all its uncertainties, doubts and
ambiguities. We do well to see them dancing together again in
a truly meaningful world.

2021

Beloved Immoralist

ONE MAN'S LOVE
OF A FICTIONAL CHARACTER

To forgive is wisdom, to forget is genius.

—GULLEY JIMSON

My FATHER'S PAINT BOX was made of leather-covered wood, worn at the corners so the wood showed through. As a child, I loved opening that box, looking at the inner compartments intended for tubes of oil paint, now crazed with dried blotches. The paints were long gone when, decades ago, I lifted the lid and looked inside, but I could see lines where brushes had lain in a mess of creativity. My father had not struck me as a man capable of mess, but he was.

For a time he painted with steady application, though the only pictures I ever saw were small studies, a crude self-portrait of a red-haired man smoking a pipe, a sparsely-furnished room with an electric lamp. All very stiffly done, but I recognized him in the effort, the thing started and left unfinished.

All his life, my father tried one sort of creativity after another. He made jewelry, he built gardens, he began a novel, writing from back to front without ever reaching the beginning. Some of these things remained after his death, but my own life of constant movement has meant abandoning most possessions, like those bits of furniture left behind by covered wagons on the western pilgrimage. Now that I live in Australia, on the far side of the planet from where I was born, there is no trail across the Pacific where I might rediscover that paint box, those crude little paintings. They are lost forever.

For some people, the objects of a life, identifying heirlooms that tell family stories or somehow hold the past together in one coherent place, remain a comfort, even a necessity. For the rest of us, these objects and places live only in memory's imaginal realm. They can no longer be turned in the hand or searched for evidence. They are ghosts. Immigrants or refugees, we live like survivors of flood and fire, with the clothes on our backs and whatever possessions a new life affords us. Still, even when we deny their necessity, the lost things call out to us. They are the future as well as the past, emblems of the final letting go.

It is my father himself I would rather have kept. Maybe that is why people hang onto old things from the past—because they *can*. The fact that I could not only reminds me, quietly, daily, what those things mean.

A MAN DIES, but a character lives. A man seldom wishes to be a character, but he becomes one anyway, the moment he is recalled. At the end, the spark of my father's character gave only the faintest light. A restless spirit was reduced to something less than infancy, tinged with paranoia. "I'm in hell," he said from somewhere in the depths of dementia. Before then, what a character! A psychic adventurer, whose story arc moved from sailor to psychiatrist to an architect of whimsy, from the Boy Scouts to LSD—Naval officer in World War II, socialist and devotee of communes, the Great Depression crashing the party of the 1960s. And most curious of all, perhaps, a man without a metaphorical mind who could still be influenced by literature. He was a man who, at least for a time, fell in love with a fictional character.

The character was a notorious artist, Gulley Jimson, from Joyce Cary's novel, *The Horse's Mouth* (1944). Cary is now nearly as forgotten as my father's paint box, but in his lifetime he was considered one of the century's major novelists. He was a marvelous writer whose career sits uncomfortably among the tastes and demands of our own time. Yet it is worth knowing about Joyce Cary and his world. Riches reside there that we should not entirely lose. I think of those lost men—Joyce Cary, Gulley Jimson, my father—and a new relation occurs in their connection. The correspondence of art and life is what I would consider here in their parallel stories, what is worth keeping and what must be left by the trail.

One of the few possessions I retain from my life in America is my father's copy of *The Horse's Mouth*. Published in paperback in 1957 by Grosset's Universal Library, it cost $1.45. Inside the front cover I find my father's signature: JC Mason. JC—like Joyce Cary, like Jesus Christ. His name was James Cameron Mason. The first name calls up memories of an urbane British actor and movie star with a voice like ironized velvet. Cameron came from our Scottish ancestors, mostly coal miners, one of whom got himself killed in the California Gold Rush (burned alive by a claim jumper, according to family lore). My father's name married Old and New World stories, a connection to the larger history of the United States, a mix of working-class roots and the veneer of aristocracy. But my father was not born to be an artist. He would strive in the American way and rebel against that striving and seek new purpose among the cultural upheavals of his time.

He was born the eldest of four sons in Trinidad, Colorado, just north of the New Mexican border. His father, Abraham Mason, had also grown up in that town of dry buttes and mesas in the valley of the Purgatory River. Abe ran away to cut timber in Idaho when he was young, then joined a Scots Canadian Regiment, the Seaforth Highlanders, fighting in World War I. He was wounded at Amiens, late in the conflict, and came home to marry a girl from Washington State. Her name was Ethel and she was older, funnier, willing to live with him in the high desert of Trinidad. They had a spirited marriage, punctuated by Abe's occasional drunkenness and fights the locals called "Mexican riots." He loved to hang out with ranchers and businessmen, telling their tall tales. The Masons were small businessmen. Abe's father, George, got his start running one of the notorious company stores that cheated coal miners in the area around Ludlow, where the infamous massacre of striking immigrants by units of the National Guard took place in 1914. By that time, George Mason had another business, a dairy known for its ice cream. He converted it to a small candy factory, and when his son came home from war he taught him the business. They made sweet things and sold them throughout Southern Colorado, New Mexico, and parts of Oklahoma and Kansas. Abe was a drummer, selling on the road, before he took over the company. The business was modestly successful, less so after the Depression, so the family always seemed to be striving and never quite arriving at the American Dream.

Trinidad is still, for my money, one of the great American small towns. Located on the old Santa Fe Trail, it seems more a part of New Mexican than Coloradan culture, with its deep Latino and Indian history and the classic mesa, Fisher's Peak, rising to the southeast. Kit Carson hung out there. The train robber, Black Jack, was hanged in the street and his head fell off—I used to stare at photos of the hanging in the local museum, trying to see that head. The charming gunfighter Bat Masterson was briefly town marshal, 1882–83, voted out due to his corruption. In some ways small and isolated, the town also feels connected to the rest of the world, surprisingly multicultural. The coal mines brought in immigrants from all over the world, and the two cemeteries, Catholic and Protestant, comprise a United Nations of the dead. Italian immigrants brought their own culinary riches and criminal ways, but so did the Anglos who competed for business in the streets. Many of those streets were paved with bricks you can still see under patches of modern asphalt. In the Roaring Twenties, Chicago gangsters like Baby Face Nelson had getaway cabins in the country nearby, especially at Stonewall Gap on the banks of the Purgatory. For a while Abe, as a local businessman, felt it necessary to carry a pistol in self-defense. Mexicans and Anglos tolerated each other and sometimes mixed. I remember a Spanish-language movie theater in town, the strong flavor of chilis in everyone's cooking, the houses with their Navajo blankets, the arrowheads my father picked up in Dust Bowl days when the topsoil blew away and left such artifacts exposed.

Jim Mason grew up with some social standing. The Mason boys all had red hair and muscular frames and were known to be good-looking, hard-working fellows, Jim the best-looking and hardest-working of them all. He had the proverbial newspaper route and sold magazines. He pinched pennies whenever he could. Sometime in the 1970s I visited my grandmother in Trinidad. I was a college student then, and wanted to know more about why my parents had divorced. Ethel was a talker, a small beautiful woman whose top-heavy bosom seemed out of proportion to the rest of her, with her thin legs and arthritic hips. She and I sat up late playing Spite and Malice, her favorite card game, trading theories.

Why had Jim, the eldest and most responsible and most successful of the Mason boys, suddenly abandoned all responsibility, leaving his wife and sons in Bellingham, Washington, for a new life in Seattle?

"Let me show you something," Ethel said.

She went into the bedroom where, since Abe's death at age 73, she slept alone, and emerged with a little notebook my father had kept as a boy.

"Take a look at this."

What I read was my father's list of his responsibilities and aspirations, the images of what he thought a good young man should be. I recognized it immediately as the very thing I had been reading in a college classroom, in *The Great Gatsby*. It's the scene after the murder, when Nick Carraway meets Gatsby's father. I no longer possess my father's notebook, but I have a copy of *Gatsby* I bought in Hobart, Tasmania. Nick tells of the father trying to piece together the strange life of the son:

He seemed reluctant to put away the picture, held it for another minute, lingeringly, before my eyes. Then he returned the wallet and pulled from his pocket a ragged old copy of a book called *Hopalong Cassidy*.

"Look here, this is a book he had when he was a boy. It just shows you."

He opened it at the back cover and turned it around for me to see. On the last fly-leaf was printed the word SCHEDULE, and the date September 12, 1906. And underneath:

Rise from bed	6.00	A.M.
Dumbbell exercise and wall-scaling	6.15–6.30	"
Study electricity, etc.	7.15–8.15	"
Work	8.30–4.30	P.M.
Baseball and sports	4.30–5.00	"
Practice elocution, poise, and how to attain it	5.00–6.00	"
Study needed inventions	7.00–9.00	"

GENERAL RESOLVES

No wasting time at Shafters or [a name, indecipherable]
No more smokeing or chewing.
Bath every other day
Read one improving book or magazine per week
Save $5.00 [crossed out] $3.00 per week
Be better to parents

This is almost exactly what I remember reading in my father's notebook. My father was Jay Gatsby, minus the bootlegging fortune. More precisely, Jay Gatsby grew out of the American ideals of his time, all the striving Horatio Algers, the dutiful self-improvers, the good boys who would discipline themselves and do right, who were also of course, boys utterly torn by their own sexual urges, their masturbation and mockery of masturbation, their fear of their fathers and terror of becoming their fathers. No wonder Jim Mason was an Eagle Scout. No wonder he studied engineering as a means to the middle class. He was a son of the Dust Bowl who kept his sexual abuse by an elderly neighbor entirely hidden, who polished his virtue and, when war broke out, applied for an appointment to the Naval Academy. He was the boy-hero of Trinidad, Colorado, Annapolis Class of '44, but shipped out in '43 because so many officers had been lost fighting the Japanese.

A laptop can carry a lot of memory, and as I type I call up details written for my father's memorial service in 2003. They pertain to a certain adventurous spirit he never lost until dementia took it from him. He was a sailor and mountaineer all his life, briefly a pilot as well, and those adventures began in his youth. By the time he was sixteen, he had already done a lot of hitchhiking up and down the Front Range of the Rockies. He and his high school friends climbed Mount Blanca, a prominent peak in the Sangre de Cristo range, in their hobnailed boots, using an old clothesline for belay. In that summer of 1937, holding down a job in Albuquerque, he got his student pilot's license. He wrote home a good account of what it was like to fly a bi-plane:

> At about 1500 ft. [Bill Cutter] gave me full control and told me to aim at a mountain. I gained 1000 ft. in a few minutes and Bill told me to lower the nose. After aiming at mountains and holding my course for a while, I got used to it. Then he told me to make a right turn. I made a floppy one with my nose too

low. I tried again and did better. After several right and left banks aimed at a mountain, I made a complete circle back to the mountain and then I reversed controls. . . . Did this several times. Then he told me to shut off the motor and glide. I banked the plane several times in the glide and kept gunning the motor so that it wouldn't cool off too quick.

This was only Jim's second time in a plane, but he reports landing safely and loving flight.

In 1939, a high school senior with dreams of Annapolis and the Navy, Jim went back to an old diary he used to keep, recording, "I have been quarrelsome, foolish and inalert today. I have had little exercise of any kind. I must have some freedom soon." The self-accusation and desire for freedom were pincers he lived between all his life. Something happened to him in the war that left a deep scar on his rectitude, not to mention his soul.

As a young lieutenant on the *USS Terry*, a Fletcher-class destroyer in Admiral Halsey's fleet, Jim saw action in many of the biggest sea battles of the Pacific war, including the Solomon Islands campaign and the "Great Marianas Turkey Shoot" that destroyed much of the Japanese fleet. He survived Typhoon Cobra in December 1944, a storm that sank three ships and damaged some twenty-seven others. Years later, after sailing through a storm in the North Pacific in a fisher-processor, I bragged to my father that I never got seasick. He saw at once I was lying but didn't admonish me for it. He just smiled—"That a fact?"—and let the subject drop.

The *Terry*'s service was nearly ended at Iwo Jima, on March 1, 1945. After days supporting the Marine landing, escorting supply ships and exchanging fire with Japanese batteries on shore, they were moving to a new position off Kitama Point on the island's north coast. A shore battery opened fire at dawn, quickly found their range, and scored a direct hit on the *Terry*'s starboard deck. The explosion killed ten sailors, wounded nineteen others, and left the ship unable to steer and without telephone communications. That morning, Jim Mason, the Eagle Scout from Trinidad, Colorado, was on the bridge as Officer of the Deck, since his skipper had gone behind to catch some sleep. He was twenty-four years old, and would always think the hit was somehow his fault, though he made the right moves to evade more damage while other ships took out the battery. He never talked about it when I was growing up, showing the veteran's usual reticence, occasionally joking that they'd lost their water supply and had to live on Coca-Cola till they got away. But in old age, as the dementia descended, so did the unstoppable memories, the terror of "Japs," the images of body parts on a deck awash in blood, a man's severed penis among them.

On a website listing the *Terry*'s dead and wounded, I find my father's name. Never in his life did he say he had been wounded in battle, and I never saw a Purple Heart among his belongings. He did mention once that his ears bled after an explosion, and perhaps that is what the website refers to. In any case, he lived with his survivor's guilt and his war trauma and for decades maintained his Gatsby-esque disguise—the successful American male, the small-town boy who triumphed over adversity and made good, the doctor who acquired enough money to take care of his parents, the dutiful older son.

ALEC GUINNESS PLAYED Gulley Jimson in the 1958 movie of *The Horse's Mouth*. He also wrote the script, which has its moments, though the picture does not entirely hold up. The whole thing is much too cute, confusing pre-war bohemians with post-war beatniks. While the novel lingers lovingly over characters like Gulley's former partner, Sara Monday, the movie sketches them as comic types, shying away from depths Joyce Cary never denied. Gulley is a difficult character to portray, a genuine artist whose devotion to his work sets him at odds with conventional society, not in some adolescent rebellion but out of a primal urge, the creative spirit itself, a force that cannot be stopped without killing the soul. His muse is the poet William Blake—lines of visionary poetry punctuate the novel almost like emanations from Jimson's own mind, so the artist's urges are nearly religious in their devotion.

Gulley lives on society's margins. If he were to do otherwise, his work would be impossible. He is not unappreciated, and by the novel's opening his paintings are selling for good prices, but he himself is just out of jail, and he finds his old life entirely overturned:

> When I came back, there was nothing. Wife and kids had gone back to her mama. Flat let to people who didn't even know my name. And the studio was a coal store. As for the Living God, my drawings, cartoons, ladders, they'd just melted. I hadn't expected to see the frypan and kettle again. You can't leave things like that about for a month in any friendly neighborhood and expect to find them in the same place. But the Living God with his stretchers and stiffeners weighed a couple of hundredweight. When I came back from gaol even the smell had gone.

Gulley keeps encountering the fearful deadeners Blake warned us about, forces pitted against the creative spirit, anti-life because they deny the darkness as well as the light, the full range of experience. Jimson's inner life is in part a constant dialogue with a dead poet. He's living with ghosts:

> Yes, I thought, there's Billy again. Handing me the truth. Even when I wouldn't take it. That's what he was saying all his life. A tear is an intellectual thing. And a joy. It's wisdom in vision. It's the prophetic eye in the loins. The passion of intelligence.

Gulley is constantly going out, away from people, "to get room for my grief." But he's drawn back by loquaciousness and even love, the detached love of an artist for whom every observation might serve the painting.

Joyce Cary writes Gulley Jimson's character so well that he never seems sentimentalized as merely the artist-rebel. He is deeply devoted, but he is also cruel to others, a liar and manipulator in the service of the truth, quite possibly a bigamist. The grubby textures of his life feel entirely and uncomfortably real. "Only individuals exist," he tells a young devotee, "—lying low in their own rat-holes. As far apart as free drinks." Gulley's rebellion against group-think at times takes on prophetic anger:

> "One man is a living soul, but two men are an indiarubber milking machine for a beer engine, and three men are noises off and four men are an asylum for cretins and five men are a committee and twenty-five are a meeting, and after that you get to the mummy-house at the British Museum, and the Sovereign People and Common Humanity and the Average and the Public and the Majority and the Life Force and Statistics and the Economic Man brainless, eyeless, wicked spawn of the universal toad sitting in the black bloody ditch of eternal night and croaking for its mate which is the spectre of Hell."

The man can *talk*.

That last passage is one of several my father marked in his copy of the book, a ballpoint line drawn lightly in the margin. Did he approve of Gulley's ideas, or only his gusto? I do not know. My father was at times an angry man—angry about America's constant warring, its betrayal of its own ideals, angry about the social hypocrisies we all encounter in a life. Anger blows through us like strong wind. I sense that Joyce Cary himself shared many of his characters' views, but not all of them, since *The Horse's Mouth* is the final volume of a trilogy, each novel narrated by a different character. The first book, *Herself Surprised* (1941), belongs to Sara Monday, a tragic presence in *The Horse's Mouth*, where she can't let go of a painting

Gulley wants returned to him. Their relationship has become an end-of-life stand-off, full of jaded love. "I'm only fit for a warning," Sara says.

"Don't say that, Sara." I said, giving her another squeeze. And meaning it. For you couldn't help liking the old trout. The very way she was speaking; easy from her soul as a jug runs when you tilt it to a wet lip; it made me tingle all over; it made me laugh and sing in the calves of my legs. It made my toes curl and my fingers itch at the tops. It made me want to go bozo with the old rascal. What a woman. The old original. Clear as a glass-eye and straight as her own front. The very way she worked her great cook's hand, jointed like a lobster, round her glass; and lolled her head on one side, and turned up her eyes and heaved up her bosom when she sighed, enjoying the feel of herself inside her stays; it made me want to squeeze her till she squealed.

Those touches of objectification, the very precision of the writing, are hardly the stuff approved by our more puritanical contemporaries. But Sara is not merely objectified, even from Gulley's point of view. She is as fully realized, as precisely rendered, as a character in fiction can be. There are no angels in Joyce Cary's trilogy, only human beings seen from different angles. Cary despised the very idea of allegory, even while thinking his characters representative of life's various urges. He was trying to convey an enlarged and entirely embodied vision of human spirit.

Yet my father only ever read the one book in the trilogy, only Gulley's point of view. He never read Sara's story, nor that of another lover, the conservative lawyer Tom Wilcher in *To Be a Pilgrim* (1942), nor could he have known the larger context of Sara's abuse by successive men or the tragic vision of her own aging body. "Out of Exile," Brad Leithauser's marvelous essay about Joyce Cary (*New York Review of Books*, June 12,

1986), points out that Gulley shouldn't be seen only as he is presented in *The Horse's Mouth*:

> Not until he is meshed into the rest of the trilogy, with its presentations of other, quieter virtues, does his depth emerge; Gulley's impracticality, monomania, anger, and adaptability need to be set beside prudence, balance, tranquility and rigidity. And only by following Sara's story from its outset will the reader appreciate the bitter sweetness of her dealings with Gulley—an extended, troubled love affair that is perhaps the trilogy's finest achievement.

So it wasn't complexity my father sought. It was freedom. It was the dream of a creative life. Jim and Jimson—they were an odd pair.

IN HIGH SCHOOL I used to take the bus from Bellingham to Seattle in order to visit Jim. He had moved out when I was twelve. I was fifteen when my parents divorced. He had also left his practice as a pediatrician in order to train as a psychiatrist, and in the years afterward I was constantly meeting mothers who missed "Dr. Jim" and fervently wished he had never left, as if they were all a bit in love with him. But something in his years of working with those parents, those children, had made him believe he should be helping families in a different way, helping them heal their dealings with each other. In the 1970s he was caught up in all the profession's revolutionary movements, every single one of them, each with its guru. I remember watching Fritz Perls videos of gestalt therapy in Jim's medical student apartment. He read every new book about undoing the buttoned-down psyche, beginning his new career trying to understand how families went wrong. *What about us?* I used to think. Why didn't he stick around and help *us* get healed? When he left, I wrote him a long angry letter, telling him he'd regret it, he'd grow old without family. And after he died, I read the drafts of the letter he tried to write in reply, explaining himself. He must have felt his justifications were useless, since his letter was never sent.

He was also living with a beautiful younger woman, Claire, who treated my brothers and me with gentle, unobtrusive loving. They moved into a houseboat like Gulley Jimson's, only theirs looked across Lake Union at the Space Needle. Going to Seattle to see my father meant leaving my troubled mother behind to stew in her anger and addiction, getting a release from it all, feeling I was temporarily saved and forgiven for being alive.

Jim used to tell me that he didn't want me to suffer all the guilt of responsibility he had felt when growing up. He wanted me to be free. And it was on one of those visits to see him that he let me know, because he knew I wanted to be a writer, that there was a novel he loved about a wild old artist, Gulley Jimson, and he had always wished he could be more like that wild old man.

THE EXPLOSION of a six-inch shell on the deck of a destroyer brought me to life. When the *Terry* was towed back to the shipyards of Oakland, California, my father attended a dance with young women from Mills College, and there he met a smart, vivacious girl who was also from Colorado, Evelyn Peterson, nicknamed "Pete" by all her friends. She must have carried an air of romantic sadness, since her father, a coal miner-turned-doctor, had died when she was eighteen and her mother, a Scottish immigrant and nurse, was already addicted to morphine. But Pete was also lively and funny and whip-smart. Jim and Pete fell in love. With the war ending they probably felt the world was their oyster, they could do anything. They both wanted to be professionals. He was moving away from engineering now, thinking of medical school, and she had taken an interest in psychology. In the meantime he was still a Naval officer, stationed after the war at Pearl Harbor.

In May 1946, Pete boarded a troop ship to join him there. My laptop contains scans of their telegram exchange:

DARLING SAILING TOMORROW MAY 30 I LOVE YOU=! PETE.

DARLING X WAS ASTOUNDED AND IMMEASURABLY HAPPY WHEN YOUR CABLEGRAM ARRIVED X HAVE BEEN SEARCHING MY BELONGINGS FOR THE RAB-BITS FOOT THAT BRINGS SUCH WONDERFUL LUCK X EVERYTHING IS ARRANGED X HARDLY BELIEVE THAT WEDNESDAY CAN BE SO FAR FROM SUNDAY X LOVE YOU WITH ALL MY HEART JIM

And a bit later:

DEAREST PETE STOP SO FAR UNABLE TO CLOSE DEAL WITH NINTH PIECE BAND FOR WEDNESDAY MORN-ING BUT STILL TRYING STOP HOPE YOU LIKE PINK CHAMPAGNE STOP NOW ABOUT ASKING THE SKIP-PER TO QUIT DRAGGING THE ANCHOR STOP I LOVE YOU STOP LT JC MASON

I have seen photos of my mother disembarking at Pearl with a lei around her neck and no doubt the wolf whistles of a few hundred sailors on deck. She looks like a young starlet, with her hair cut well above the shoulders as it was most of her life and her tomboyish name, yet entirely and buoyantly sexual. Another photo taken in a car shows Jim and Pete beaming for the camera like the very gods of post-war happiness. I know what it's like to be drunk on love. I also know what it's like to be drunk, and my mother was possibly a bit of both. She did like pink champagne, and pretty much anything else with alcohol in it, but her "problem" would not become appar-ent to the rest of us for another decade or two. They had married that year in Trinidad, flanked by Jim's Navy pals with raised swords.

In the 1950s my father was still in conventional hero mode, an Eisenhower Republican, a young physician looking about for a small town in which to practice. He earned his MD at Washington University in St. Louis, where my mother would get her PhD in Psychology. It must have been a heady time. Masters and Johnson were at work on their studies of sex, and at some point they invited my mother to join the study. Though she turned them down, she was a woman of strong libido, frank intelligence, and would have at least one extra-marital affair, possibly two, before my parents split.

The other big medical fashion in St. Louis at the time was the frontal lobotomy as a cure for pretty much anything that ailed people, from manic depression to drug addiction. At this point in their marriage, the big headache for Jim and Pete was her Scottish mother, Maggie, who kept getting fired from nursing jobs for stealing morphine. I do not know how the decision was reached, but Pete was persuaded that a lobotomy would cure her mother's addiction. Whether it was the then-famous Dr. Walter Jackson Freeman II, a man who graced the cover of *Time* for his innovation, or some other doctor performing the procedure (it could hardly be called a surgery), Maggie's case was not one of the rare successes. She developed a post-operative infection, ended up in a semi-vegetative state with occasional obscene ramblings, and was institutionalized for the rest of her life. I never met her, never heard her voice, and was in my forties before I learned any details of the secret guilt my mother harbored, one of the deep triggers that fired her drinking.

So the young hero from Trinidad had a brilliant, beautiful wife who could go sideways at a moment's notice. They settled in Bellingham, just under the Canadian border, then little known but still one of the most beautiful parts of the United States. My brothers and I grew up looking at mountains like

Shuksan and Baker, the lights of Vancouver BC to the north, hiking and sailing and skiing, all of us athletically assuaged by the wild. Our parents were remarkable. Pete and a partner created the first mental health clinic in the town, then she took a job teaching at the local college, on its way to becoming Western Washington University. Many years later, my younger brother took a class from her, and realized in the middle of a lecture on addiction that he was the only student in the hall who knew she was blitzed. We used to joke bitterly that she'd "rather have a bottle in front of me than a frontal lobotomy." She was able to keep the trick going until her late fifties, when her drunkenness showed and colleagues gently coaxed her to early retirement. In the early years, Jim was building his practice, but he would remember having to clean Pete's vomit off a car seat while awaiting the arrival of a prospective colleague at the airport. The drinking worsened, and whatever else tore at their marriage worsened, and we three boys (I was the middle son) cringed in solitude during their tearing fights. "I used to have this fantasy," Jim told me late in life, before the dementia got him. "I just packed her into a space capsule and blasted her off to the moon." When we heard that one, my brother and I laughed ourselves silly, a beautiful release after decades of accumulated tension. By that time Pete had been in and out of most rehab clinics in the Pacific Northwest.

By the time Jim moved to Seattle in about 1966, his politics had swerved left. Johnson's lies and Nixon's lies erased the last vestiges of the dutiful older son in him, the conservative, and he was reborn a man of distinctly socialist leanings and utopian hopes. For decades he and Claire participated in a sort of floating commune, living together without being married, meeting their fellow communards for retreats in different parts of the country. They followed a benign leader named Jack Gibb whose ideas arose from theories of organizational development. Jack believed that communities flourished when they emphasized trust over fear. He was quite right, of course, and in my own life I have seen institutional fear making life miserable for people time and time again. The one small problem for the "Trust Group," as I came to call them, was that they could rarely accomplish practical living together for more than a few weeks at a time. The necessity of having jobs and making money kept them apart, and they were unable to make Jack's theories work in the production of saleable products or otherwise earning a living. They had the spirit right, but the market defeated them, as it does most utopian ventures.

On the few occasions when I joined the Trust Group for one of their retreats, I felt myself out of step with them, unable to let go or open myself to the fluid sexual promise some of its members offered to me. My problem was something none of them had ever experienced. I wanted to be an artist, a writer, which meant holding my nose to the grindstone, working more than enjoying free love. And herein lies the paradox of Gulley Jimson that perhaps my father did not entirely understand. He saw the freedom of the artist, the wildness and irresponsibility, the way his life remains unintelligible to other people because he simply does not share their motives and desires. But he might not have seen that Gulley was also a deeply disciplined man, a man who made ambitious canvases and put his life on the line to finish them, a man for whom freedom was not entirely personal. Jim had been an engineer and a doctor. He loved literature, but did not think metaphorically. When I began to publish poetry, he was curious about it all. Late in life he even took a poetry class, amazed to find that the textbook used was one his middle son had edited.

Jim's experiments were not in making art, but in making a life. He must have been in his sixties when he hiked into the Cascades with two friends and tried LSD. His ecstatic notes from the trip are among the many personal possessions I have lost in my wanderings. Of course, lots of artists experiment with drugs and alcohol, and some even survive the damage that can result, but whatever my own minor chemical dabblings, I was always more focused on being able to work, even if most of what I wrote seemed a pale shadow of what I dreamed.

It's a strange thing, trying to make art in a country like America, where people do not believe you are working unless you have a conventional job with benefits and the rest. Even now, in my new life as a retired academic writing full-time in Tasmania, I sometimes feel that neighbors do not believe I am working. They think I've got nothing to do and might enjoy partying late into the night. But I am not really a free man in that sense. I am chained to my craft, thinking of it even when I'm out chopping wood or clearing brush on our block of land near the Southern Ocean. There is something I want to finish before I die.

At least, I think, I am not chained to conventional ideas of what I should be doing. But perhaps we are all chained to something, if not to each other. After twenty-odd years of living together, Jim and Claire shocked their friends by getting married. They were an ideal couple, their friends argued. Why ruin it?

JOYCE CARY'S PATH as a writer was a crooked one, and success came late. Unlike Gulley, he was a man of utmost integrity, a family man who loved his wife and children, but like Gulley he was a deliberate artist even in his failures. He was born in Northern Ireland in 1888, the same year as T. S. Eliot, and his parents moved the family soon after to London. He grew up an Englishman with a strong sense of his Irish heritage and divided sympathies. Cary found his vocation young, quitting school at seventeen and heading off to Paris and Edinburgh to study art. This is why he was able to make Gulley's obsessions as a painter so vivid and real, casting them in relief also through other people's eyes. Here is Gulley talking about painting with his friend Cokey:

"Half a minute of revelation is worth a million years of know nothing." "Who lives a million years?" "A million people every twelve months. I'll show you how to look at a picture, Cokey. Don't look at it. Feel it with your eye." "I'm not a snail, am I?" "And first you feel the shapes in the flat—the patterns, like a carpet." "You told me that one before." "And then you feel it in the round." "All that fat." "Not as if it were a picture of anyone. But a coloured and raised map. You feel all the rounds, the smooths, the sharp edges, the flats and hollows, the lights and shades, the cools and warms. The colours and textures. There's hundreds of little differences all fitting together." "The bath towel isn't too bad, I can see that—it's got the look of huckaback." "And then you feel the bath, the chair, the towel, the carpet, the bed, the jug, the window, the fields and the woman as themselves. But not as any old jug and woman. But the jug of jugs and the woman of women. You feel jugs are like that and you never knew it before. . . . A jug can be a door if you open it. And a work of imagination opens it for you. And then you feel with all the women that ever lived and all the women that are ever going to live, and you feel their feeling while they are alone with themselves—in some chosen private place, bathing, drying, dressing, criticizing, touching, admiring themselves safe behind locked doors. Nothing there but women's feeling and woman's beauty and critical eye."

When texts are read primarily for their virtue or lack of virtue, we miss out on Cary's particularity, his desire to let things and people be themselves. Humanity, seen this way, might well be compromised by all the systems of injustice, but we shouldn't throw it out entirely in our pursuit of the good because it is itself a kind of goodness, a kind of love.

Literature got ahold of Cary young, particularly the writing of James Joyce and D. H. Lawrence. He abandoned his art studies and went to Oxford, ending with a fourth-class degree that offered him few professional opportunities. After service in the Red Cross during the Balkan Wars, he joined the Nigerian Colonial Service in 1913 and spent the next seven years in that country, taking part in the African campaigns of World War I. He was wounded in battle in 1915—wounded in the ear, in fact, a weird rhyme with my father's war. On leave home he married a beautiful woman, Gerty Ogilvie, started a family, and was still trying to write with little success. Aside from the excellent novel *Mr. Johnson* (1939, filmed by Bruce Beresford in 1990), little of Cary's African fiction is read now. Even his humane, generous sympathies can seem patronizing in post-colonial readings. Cary's publisher kept him on more as an esteemed literary status symbol than for sales. *The Horse's Mouth*, and especially the movie with Alec Guinness, changed all that. After decades of toil, Cary had pulled off the difficult trick of being both literary in the most ambitious way and popular.

He was a writer of loving particularity, suspicious of symbolic structures. His theme was the creative impulse of life itself, nature itself, a freedom that today might well be frowned upon by those committed to the idea that social justice is the only worthy goal. Looking back on his career in *The Saturday Review* (May 28, 1955), he wrote,

> Because we are free creative souls, for ever inventing, achieving, we live in a world of continuous revolution, continuous change. . . . The personal tragedies of ruined men, superseded business, frustrated artists, can be mitigated by various devices, but the fundamental insecurity, the fundamental conflict remain. To the free personal soul we owe all love, beauty, everything that makes life worth living; and also that everlasting conflict and insecurity that makes it tragic. Freedom is all our joy and all our pain.

Less than two years after that article appeared, Joyce Cary was dead, aged 68, following a slow, crippling descent into motor neuron disease—what Americans call Lou Gehrig's disease after another of our heroes.

MY FATHER LOVED living in his body. All his life he was fit and active. When he left the houseboat for work he would walk up the steep city staircases to a clinic on Seattle's Capitol Hill, and on his return at the end of the day he would loosen his tie, take off his shoes, and step onto his windsurfer for a quick sail across Lake Union. Visits to the houseboat were always a deep relief. We would swim in the lake or sit in the tiny living room, looking across at the city and talking about damned near anything, especially the latest experiments in living Jim and Claire were pursuing. In one of those conversations I was shocked to hear him recalling sexual abuse, how an old man who lived in a neighboring house in Trinidad had invited Jim and his friends inside, then had somehow made them let him suck their cocks. I remember the chill of denial in my own bones, and how he too must have felt shocked by the revelation and never mentioned it again. But there it was, this conflict between our ideal images of ourselves and the reality of our experience, the very thing Joyce Cary dramatized so movingly in his best fiction.

Alzheimer's ran in Jim's family, and he feared it above all deaths. He used to tell us he would rather get into his kayak and paddle out to sea and disappear. Or he would die like Socrates, gather his friends around for a final talk, then drink the hemlock. He studied the methods of the Hemlock Society, and when the first signs of aphasia came he made his best friend promise to eventually help him die.

By the time his disease was so advanced that he no longer knew us, no longer knew even how to eat his food, we had all taken turns with him, wiping his bum and the rest of what care-givers regularly do, the things Claire did with such loving patience for years. When I heard him say "I'm in hell," I could no longer determine whether or not the words were connected to what we call, for lack of a better word, reality.

Did he recognize any of us? Did some part of him know the shadows who surrounded him? I remember him pointing to a photograph of my older brother, who had died in a mountaineering accident, and holding a fist over his heart. What did he see of us before he died and we scattered his ashes with my brother's in the mountains?

The character he loved, Gulley Jimson, shared with Jim the medical condition of hypertension, and always suspected he would go of a stroke. At the end of *The Horse's Mouth*, that's exactly what happens, despite the old painter's unyielding spirit:

> "Please don't talk," said the nun. "That's all right, mother," I said, "they can't hear me because of the noise of the traffic and because they aren't listening. And it wouldn't make any difference if they did. They're too young to learn, and if they weren't they wouldn't want to." "It's dangerous for you to talk, you're very seriously ill." "Not so seriously as you're well. How don't you enjoy life, mother. I should laugh all around my neck at this minute if my shirt wasn't a bit on the tight side." "It would be better for you to pray." "Same thing, mother."

In the movie Alec Guinness gets on a boat and heads out to sea on the Thames—more the way my father wished he could go. But that's the way of things in this world. We don't always get our wish.

2021

PART TWO

Voices, Dead and Living

The Freedom of Montaigne

These essays are an attempt to communicate a soul.

—Virginia Woolf

Only fools are cocksure.

—Michel de Montaigne

In a book of essays, why not celebrate the greatest essayist of them all?

The soul selects her own Montaigne, and nearly every soul can find the Montaigne she needs. Especially in terrible times, we look to him for ordinary sanity in extraordinary prose. Immune to idealism, he invented his wonderful *essais* from a seemingly complete being. "The soul that entertains philosophy," he wrote, "ought by its health to render the body beautiful too."* He loved health but hated doctors, and there's

---

*Unless otherwise indicated, translations are from the Modern Library *Montaigne: Selected Essays* (1949). Revised and edited, and with an introduction by Blanchard Bates, and translated by Charles Cotton and William Hazlitt. This is the battered paperback I happened to have on hand while traveling through America. Since then, I've also come to admire M. A. Screech's translation of *The Complete Essays* (Penguin 2003), and I'm told that Donald Frame's translations (Stanford University Press 1958) also deserve study.

something therapeutic about reading him in barbarous times. He was steeped in philosophy, yet, as William Hazlitt wrote, "he did not set up for a philosopher, wit, orator, or moralist, but he became all these by merely daring to tell us whatever passed through his mind, in its naked simplicity and force."

In an unsigned review published in 1925, T. S. Eliot argued, "Montaigne is just the sort of writer to provide a stimulant to a poet; for what the poet looks for in his reading is not a philosophy—not a body of doctrine or even a consistent point of view which he endeavours to *understand*—but a point of departure." He had Shakespeare in mind, but also himself. In the same decade, Virginia Woolf reviewed a new edition of the essays:

> . . . this talking of oneself, following one's own vagaries, giving the whole map, weight, colour, and circumference of soul in its confusion, its variety, its imperfection—this art belonged to one man only: to Montaigne.

It's hard even in our jaded generation not to be similarly wowed. The essays Montaigne wrote between 1572 and his death twenty years later are unlike anything else I have read—a book of one man and a book of the world. They present textual problems because of their author's technique of revision and accrual over three editions—making new pearls out of old irritations—but they delight because of the breadth and brightness of his being. He allowed for contradiction and contrariness. "We are, I know not how," Montaigne wrote, "double in ourselves." W. H. Auden would borrow that line for *The Double Man* (1941), his verse dissection of modern psychology and history. Woolf, too, had noted these inner and outer realms:

> For beyond the difficulty of communicating oneself, there is the supreme difficulty of being oneself. The soul, or life within us, by no means agrees with the life outside us. If one has the courage to ask her what she thinks, she is always saying the very opposite of what other people say.

We are at liberty to discover more than one Montaigne, including the political freethinker who saw beyond the sectarian wars of his own century to something like our postcolonial perspective. As Woolf put it,

> Again with politics, statesmen are always praising the greatness of Empire, and preaching the moral duty of civilizing the savage. But look at the Spanish in Mexico, cried Montaigne in a burst of rage. "So many cities levelled with the ground, so many nations exterminated . . . and the richest and most beautiful part of the world turned upside down for the traffic of pearl and pepper! Mechanic victories!"

No wonder we call him our contemporary. Montaigne was a man of the Renaissance, but he speaks powerfully to our own era of religious division, tribalism, and global instability.

Readers dismayed by current politics should read Montaigne's essay "Of Cruelty":

> Among other vices I cruelly hate cruelty, both by nature and judgment, as the extreme of all vices. But it is to such a degree of softness that I cannot see a chicken's neck slit without trouble, and I cannot bear to hear the cry of a hare beneath the teeth of my dogs, though the chase is a stirring pleasure.

Our terrorists and torturers would not have surprised him. He lived through the St. Bartholomew's Day Massacre and other Christian atrocities, witnessed plenty of killing and public execution. His love of beauty and poetry arose partly in response to the cruelty surrounding him:

> I live in a time wherein we abound in incredible examples of this vice through the license of our civil wars; and we see nothing in ancient histories more extreme than what we experience every day. But that has not at all accustomed me to

it. I could hardly persuade myself, before I had seen it with my eyes, that there could be found men so monstrous who would wish to commit murder for the sole pleasure of it, would hack and lop off limbs of others, sharpen their wits to invent unusual torments and new kinds of deaths, without hatred, without profit, and for the sole end of enjoying the pleasant spectacle of the pitiful gestures and motions, the lamentable groans and cries of a man dying in anguish.

Montaigne can be funny and beautiful as well as outraged, but he is never deluded about the world. It is what it is, and the human part of it appalls as much as it edifies.

Many have made their own Montaigne. Escaping Nazism in World War II, the Jewish writer Stefan Zweig found solace in the *Essays*. Here I turn to Sarah Bakewell's excellent book, *How to Live: or A Life of Montaigne in One Question and Twenty Attempts at an Answer* (2010). Bakewell quotes a letter Zweig wrote to a friend from his "enforced exile in South America":

The similarity of [Montaigne's] epoch and situation to ours is astonishing. I am not writing a biography; I propose simply to present as an example his fight for interior freedom.

To Bakewell, Zweig's essay represents the usefulness of Montaigne for readers of vastly different historical periods. She writes,

In a time such as that of the Second World War, or in civil-war France . . . ordinary people's lives are sacrificed to the obsessions of fanatics, so the question for any person of integrity becomes not so much "How do I survive?" as "How do I remain fully human?" The question comes in many variants: How do I preserve my true self? How do I ensure that I go no further in my speech or actions than I think is right? How do I avoid losing my soul? Above all: How do I remain free?

Montaigne was no freedom fighter in the usual sense, Zweig admits. "He has none of the rolling tirades and the beautiful verve of a Schiller or Lord Byron, none of the aggression of a Voltaire." His constant assertions that he is lazy, feckless, and irresponsible make him sound a poor hero, yet these are not really failings at all. They are essential to his battle to preserve his particular self as it is.

Zweig committed suicide with his wife in 1942. Bakewell points out that he had selected "a very Stoic Montaigne," as if clinging to the *Essays* for survival. She offers Zweig's distillation of Montaigne into "eight freedoms":

Be free from vanity and pride.
Be free from belief, disbelief, convictions, and parties.
Be free from habit.
Be free from ambition and greed.
Be free from family and surroundings.
Be free from fanaticism.
Be free from fate; be master of your own life.
Be free from death; life depends on the will of others, but death on our own will.

Montaigne knew that death should not be feared, but that the fearful anticipation of death can be agony. That's why we must find a way to live with our death, to accept it in the fullness of living.

I DEVOURED SARAH BAKEWELL's best-selling book partly in procrastination while slogging through a very different biography. Philippe Desan's weighty, authoritative tome appeared in France in 2014 as *Montaigne: Une biographie politique.** If Mon-

---

Montaigne: A Life. Philippe Desan. Trans. Steven Rendall and Lisa Neal. Princeton: Princeton University Press, 2017.

taigne's renewed popularity owes something to books like Bakewell's, Desan disdains the popular, and would give us Montaigne in his own time. He takes his time doing it, too, and I can't blame the translators for the merely functional prose style and a scholar's obsession with minutiae. His declared goal "is to relate the two inseparable aspects of [Montaigne's] life: literature and political action." Desan belabors details about the workings of French regional government in the sixteenth century. We who read Montaigne for help in our trying times, Desan suggests, ought to see him clearly in relation to his own. Fair enough. Montaigne was a Catholic aristocrat, though some of his family turned Protestant and he had friends on both sides. He was a councillor and mayor of Bordeaux, a friend of kings and princes who somehow survived an epoch of bloody religious conflict, retired in relative peace to his books and died of natural causes in his bed at 59. If many of his views and curiosities now seem to us liberal in the best sense of that word, he had his conservative, pragmatic side as well.

It was one hell of a century—the Renaissance bleeding into the Reformation, with occasional rashes of plague and burnings at the stake. Twenty years before Montaigne's birth in 1533, Machiavelli published *The Prince*. In the year of Montaigne's death, Shakespeare produced *Richard III*. It was the century in which Copernicus and Brahe disturbed the universe, in which Da Vinci died and Cortez conquered New Spain, in which Suleiman the Magnificent brought the Ottoman Empire nearly to Vienna, in which Tyndale died for his Bible, in which Anne Boleyn and Mary Queen of Scots lost their heads and the Armada sailed for England. And that's not the half of it. One could be excused for feeling the earth unsteady beneath one's feet.

If a man had to make his place in the world and a woman had to make a good marriage, it helped to have successful parents. Montaigne's mother was a tough, controlling figure, but he was loyal to her, and he adored his father, who had been a soldier and politician and valued education above all things. His great essay "On the Education of Children," composed as a letter to Madame Diane de Foix, begins, "I never saw a father who, however mangy or hunchbacked his son might be, failed to own him." For Montaigne, philosophy in its root sense was the essence of education and "that which instructs us to live." Those who disdained philosophy and went running after fact he called "ergotists." Schools become "veritable jails of imprisoned youths." Real education would educate the whole person, and the most wholly educated people were the great philosophers and poets:

> Someone asked Socrates of what country he was. He did not answer "Of Athens," but, "Of the world." Having an imagination richer and more expansive, he embraced the whole world as his city and extended his society, his friendship, and his knowledge to all mankind; not as we do, who look no farther than our feet.

His style can be energetic—the manner of expression every bit as important as the substance expressed.

> History is more my quarry, or poetry, which I love with a particular affection. For, as Cleanthes said, just as sound compressed in the narrow passage of a trumpet comes out sharper and stronger, so, it seems to me, a thought compressed into the measured harmony of verse bounds forth much more briskly and strikes me with a livelier jolt.

Convinced that too much effort was spent in giving sons the ancient languages in the formal classroom, Montaigne's father decided to raise his son from birth as a speaker of Latin:

> . . . in my infancy, and before I began to speak, he committed me to the care of a German (who since died a famous phy-

sician in France), totally ignorant of our language and very well versed in Latin. This man, whom he had sent for specially and whom he paid extremely well, had me continually with him. With him there were also two others, of less learning, to attend me and to relieve him. They conversed with me in no other language but Latin. As to the rest of the household, it was an inviolable rule that neither himself, nor my mother, nor any valet or maid should speak anything in my company but such Latin words as everyone had learned in order to gaggle with me. It is wonderful how much everyone derived from this.

Though Montaigne claims to have forgotten much of it later in formal schooling (where he got his experience of how not to educate children), his mind remained well stocked with so much classical culture that his essays are veritable anthologies of quotation and allusion. From his early reading of Ovid he learned that the first principle of reading is pleasure, and also that the world is a strange and magical place, constantly changing. It was a world in which science, superstition, and medicine melded together. In 1560, for example, Montaigne would witness the trial of Martin Guerre, or the man who pretended to be Martin Guerre. The only DNA test was hearsay and memory.

Desan covers all this very well, and with more context than Bakewell's book—though, as I say, the context sometimes seems best suited for specialists. He is particularly strong on the most important friendship of Montaigne's early years, with the poet and philosopher Estienne de La Boétie. The two young men formed an intense bond, their sympathies literary and intellectual, but also more—perhaps homoerotic. Desan writes that, in a poem by La Boétie, "Montaigne is depicted as a lost soul who chases women in brothels. More interested in sexual prowess followed by long periods of laziness, the young Montaigne represents a very different kind of friendship. . . ."

Just as La Boétie gives us a version of Montaigne, so Montaigne would preserve La Boétie's philosophical writings and leave an account of his friend's untimely death of the plague in 1563. La Boétie's discourse *On Voluntary Servitude*, which Montaigne at the very least edited and published (some believe he wrote it himself), seems to be a remarkable piece of political philosophy—though I have read of it only in the books discussed here. *On Voluntary Servitude* asks why it is that people willingly give up their liberty and devote themselves to a king: "What evil chance has so denatured man that he, the only creature really born to be free, lacks the memory of his original condition and the desire to return to it?" The work prefigures Rousseau and Locke, and it would certainly have been viewed as seditious or at least dangerous thinking in Montaigne's time. But this was also nearly the moment of Shakespeare's history plays, questioning the divine right of kings, and some form of political enlightenment was very much in the air even as monarchies were clamping down. In part La Boétie presents an aristocratic curiosity about the lower orders—like voters who cannot apprehend their own interest, but develop a crush on a strong leader. As Bakewell puts it,

> La Boétie believes that tyrants somehow hypnotize their people—though this term had not yet been invented. To put it another way, they fall in love with him. They lose their will in his. It is a terrible spectacle to see "a million men serving miserably with their necks under the yoke, not constrained by a greater force, but somehow (it seems) enchanted and charmed by the mere mention of the name of one, whose power they should not fear, since he is alone, and whose qualities they should not love, since he is savage and inhuman towards them."

Desan's reading of La Boétie is more complex. If *On Voluntary Servitude* contains a critique of tyranny, it also suggests that degrees of freedom might remain even in relinquishment. To make a comparison with our own time, the so-called "nanny state" with its Medicare for everyone might eliminate part of the free market, but it also relieves citizens of oppressive stresses. "That is why allegiance to rules established by others is not incompatible with freedom in principle," Desan writes. "To be free is to retain the possibility of emancipation, while at the same time conforming to the laws that force us into servitude." Freedom is not an absolute, not an either-or proposition, but a set of relations, possibilities mixed with actualities. The argument is less sexy than a full-on liberal or conservative thesis, but it contains a respectable dose of realism. Let us consider this again in relation to our own time. Is America freer because it has more guns, one might ask? Or is Australia, with stricter gun laws, freer because less fear-driven? Desan quotes Montaigne saying "Our truth nowadays is not what is, but what others can be convinced of." In "Of Giving the Lie," Montaigne wrote, "The first step in the corruption of morals is the banishment of truth. . . ." To which I say, *Thou shouldst be living at this hour.*

MONTAIGNE IS THE Shakespeare of the essay form, and after 1603 the Bard's plays exhibit the intoxicating influence of John Florio's wild and wonderful translation of Montaigne's work. Bakewell has some fun with this:

> Where Montaigne writes, "Our Germans, drowned in wine" (*nos Allemans, noyez dan le vin*), Florio has "our carowsing tospot German souldiers, when they are most plunged in their cups, and as drunke as Rats." A phrase which the modern translator Donald Frame renders calmly as "werewolves, goblins, and chimeras" emerges from Floriation as "Larves, Hobgoblins, Robbin-good-fellowes, and other such Bug-beares and Chimeraes"—a piece of pure *Midsummer Night's Dream.*

Montaigne wrote essays on smells, on drunkenness, on thumbs, on names, on prayer, on solitude, on books, on how "Difficulty Increases Desire" (a title translated by the magnificently named M. A. Screech). He was hard on religious hypocrites and harder on doctors, having suffered terribly from kidney stones, an affliction inherited from his father, which he wrote about in "On the Resemblance of Children to their Fathers." Part of the joy of reading him is in discovering his unfettered mind. Discouraged writers can find balm in his words:

> And even if nobody reads me, have I wasted my time in entertaining myself so many idle hours with such useful and agreeable thoughts? In modeling this figure upon myself, I have been so often obliged to shape and compose myself in order to bring myself out that the model has thereby become firm and has to some extent formed itself. Painting myself for others, I have painted my inner self in clearer colors than were my first ones. I have no more made my book than my book has made me: a book consubstantial with its author, concerned only with me, a vital part of my life; not having an outside and alien concern and objective like all other books. Have I wasted my time by taking account of myself so continually, so carefully? For they who survey themselves only in their minds, and occasionally aloud, do not examine themselves so fundamentally nor penetrate so deeply as does he who makes it his study, his work, and his trade, who with all his faith, with all his strength, binds himself to make a lasting account.

His great invention, the essay, remains an *attempt* and a field of infinite flexibility. "And, in truth," he wrote, "what are these things I scribble but grotesques and monstrous bodies pieced together of sundry members, without any definite shape, having no order, coherence, or proportion, except by accident?"

He seems curious about everything. Sometime after 1550, when fifty native Brazilians were put on display for Henry II and Catherine de Medici, Montaigne's imagination was galvanized. He could hardly stop writing about "cannibals" in contrast to the monsters of his own civilization: "The savages do not so much shock me in roasting and eating the bodies of the dead as do those who torment and persecute the living." He pitied Caliban before Caliban even dreamed:

> . . . I am sorry that, seeing so clearly into their faults, we should be so blind to our own. I conceive there is more barbarity in eating a man alive than in eating him dead, in tearing by tortures and the rack a body that is still full of feeling, in roasting him by degrees, causing him to be bitten and torn by dogs and swine . . . than in roasting and eating him after he is dead.

Montaigne was a man of his time, an aristocrat, a survivor of brutal political and religious conflict. But out of the thinking of men like him we derive the values that ended slavery and could dispel the tribalism now eating away at our world. He greets us as a brother, as a friend, and trusts us to understand how much alike we may really be in our bodies, our desires and curiosities, our flaws, our fears, our love.

2018

Digging Up Diderot

I do not flatter myself into thinking that, when the
great revolution comes, my name will still survive. . . .
But at least I will be able to tell myself that I contributed
as much as possible to the happiness of my fellow man,
and prepared, perhaps from afar, the improvement of
their lot.

— DENIS DIDEROT, *POLITICAL WRITINGS*

What is this will, what is this freedom of the man who's
dreaming?

— DENIS DIDEROT, *D'ALEMBERT'S DREAM*

AMONG THE CIVIL MINDS that teach us to read the world,
Denis Diderot deserves renewed recognition. There are at least
two Diderots, both controversial, both remarkable Enlightenment figures. The first was a renowned *philosophe* and athe-
ist associated with Voltaire and Rousseau but often thought
their inferior in accomplishment. He was known chiefly as the
major author and editor of the *Encyclopédie*—a revolutionary
project of the eighteenth century—as well as a few plays and
other works such as *Philosophical Thoughts* (1746), *The Skeptic's*

Walk (1747), and *Letter on the Blind For the Benefit of Those Who See* (1749). He also wrote a brilliantly risqué novel, *The Indiscreet Jewels* (1748), in which women's genitalia narrate their experiences. Perhaps this is the figure about whom W. H. Auden wrote, in "Voltaire at Ferney," "Dear Diderot was dull but did his best." Auden loved alliteration more than truth in that line. Diderot was anything but dull and did not always publish his best. In 1749 he spent four months in prison for his early writings, and that trauma probably shocked him into withholding some of his most significant work from publication.

The second Diderot emerged in the centuries following his death in 1784, with the discovery and publication of his major philosophical works, his most enduring fiction, and other writings. For a time he was a missing link of the Enlightenment, highly influential—directly or indirectly—on America's founders, as well as Goethe and a small army of other writers. It may be a long time before Diderot's complicated legacy is fully understood, which makes Andrew S. Curran's 2019 biography, *Diderot and the Art of Thinking Freely*, a timely exercise, especially helpful for those of us not steeped in philosophy. He humanizes Denis Diderot by uniting the public intellectual and the secret one known to his daughter and a few avid supporters. Diderot becomes a flawed, energetic man, a courageous defender of the liberated mind. He disparaged colonialism and slavery, and encouraged Catherine the Great of Russia to elevate the rule of law above "the abuses of the state and the Church"—advice she considered and set aside. In much of his best work the form of the Platonic dialogue achieves irreverent vitality and wit. His writing is, in my limited experience of some recent translations, fun to read.

Diderot was famous in Parisian circles for his conversation, so it's not surprising that his philosophy exhibits a wacky enthusiasm. *Rameau's Nephew* (written in 1761 but not published for another 130 years) reads like the love child of Socrates and Samuel Beckett with a dash of Mozartian élan. The poetry footnoted in our Plato texts finds an equivalent here in musical referents, though the ideas batted back and forth include good and evil, pleasure, and the nonexistence of God. The talkers are HIM and ME (*Lui* and *Moi*), the former being the eponymous and fictionalized relative of France's leading composer at the time:

> He's the nephew of that famous musician who delivered us from Lulli and his plain chant which we had been intoning for more than a hundred years, and who set down all those unintelligible versions and apocalyptic truths about the theory of music which neither he nor anyone else ever really understood, and who left us with a certain number of operas which have some harmony, some snatches of song, some disconnected ideas, some banging and crashing, some flights, some triumphs, some spears, some glories, some murmurings, some breathless victories, along with a few dance tunes which will last forever and which, having killed off the Florentine, will in turn be killed off by the Italian virtuosi....

I found this lively translation by Kate E. Tunstall and Caroline Warman online, and was struck again by comparisons to Beckett's flights of invective. The nephew refers to himself as "an ignoramus, a fool, a madman, an upstart, a hanger-on, what the Burgundians call a dirty scally, a cheat, a greedy pig...." He's brilliant and despairing, offering at times the absurdist minimalism of Beckett as well:

> We were both silent for a while, during which time he walked up and down, whistling and singing. To get him to talk about his talent again, I said: What are you working on at the moment?
>
> HIM — Nothing.
>
> ME — That must be very tiring.

These two men have met near the fleshpots of the Palais Royale, and converse in a well-known cafe. The work has an effervescence one doesn't often find in philosophy. Professor Curran informs us that Diderot was also satirizing his enemies in the portrait of Rameau, but this context pales beside the dialogue's comic tone. It's wonderful stuff.

Yet *Rameau's Nephew* and other masterpieces were nearly lost to us, as Curran writes:

> These hidden works did not appear in the months after Diderot died; they trickled out over the course of decades. Several of his lost books were published during the waning years of the French Revolution; others appeared during the course of the Bourbon Restoration (1814–30), while still more of his writing emerged during the Second Empire (1852–70). Perhaps the most significant addition to Diderot's corpus came in 1890 when a librarian discovered a complete manuscript version of Diderot's masterpiece, *Le neveau de Rameau* (Rameau's Nephew), in a *bouquiniste*'s stand on the banks of the Seine. In this riotous philosophical dialogue, the writer courageously gave life to an unforgettable anti-hero who extolled the virtues of evil and social parasitism while preaching the right to unbridled pleasure.

Professor Curran's prologue, "Unburying Diderot," makes the drama of representation—a phrase Diderot might have relished—only too clear. The evidence about Diderot's life is spotty and mythologized. We don't have a full biography because too much was hidden and too few letters survive. Curran's book considers its subject in thematically-arranged chapters devoted mostly to the writing. The life itself might have seemed dull, to use Auden's word, devoted as it was to the hard labor of intellectual pursuits—two decades on the *Encyclopédie* alone. But there was enough upheaval and romantic turmoil in Diderot's life to make him something of a representative man in an era when class conflict and the blindness of Europe's monarchies led to bloody, world-shattering revolutions.

IN A TIME OF religious and political intolerance, it is easy to be grateful for the Enlightenment, even with its subsequent violent idealisms. Jefferson said every generation needs its revolution, but that puts a lot of strain on the world. We need a break from it all, and surely the intellectual brilliance of figures from Newton and Locke to Diderot shouldn't be blamed for the Reign of Terror. Revolutionary fervor is its own intolerance, as we have seen again and again in modern times. Diderot was not a saint by any means—he was refreshingly human, argumentative, occasionally dishonest, funny, ribald, and enthusiastic. But he was not a particularly practical man, as his defender Catherine the Great pointed out to him during his visit to her court in St. Petersburg in 1773:

> Monsieur Diderot, I have listened with the greatest pleasure to all the inspirations flowing from your brilliant mind. But all your grand philosophies, which I understand very well, would do marvelously in books and very badly in practice. In your plans for reform, you forget the difference between our two roles: you work only on paper which consents to anything: it is smooth and flexible and offers no obstacles either to your imagination or to your pen, whereas I, poor empress, work on human skin, which is far more prickly and sensitive. (Curran)

One doesn't have to think of Buchenwald to get a chill from the "poor" empress's choice of metaphors, and one doesn't have to think of Plato's philosopher king to wonder what might have happened if Church and state had been more enlightened, more compassionate and open to change. Still, Catherine was remarkable in her support of intellectuals, providing Diderot with an income, even buying his vast personal library and moving it after his death to her capital. The Enlightenment was both opposed and fostered by the monarchies it under-mined—another of history's ironies.

Diderot's intellectual life started in the Church, and he very nearly became a canon, educated by Jesuits first in his home town of Langres, where he was born in 1713, and later in Paris. When he left the Sorbonne in 1735 he had received a deeper formal education than the other *philosophes*, studying theology and philosophy. He then mastered Italian and English and began working as a translator, with sidelines as a minor swindler and scoundrel. Both his education and his experience of intolerance—from Church, state, and his own demanding father—inspired his independence. He wouldn't have approved of the puritanical Jansenist movement among French Catholics, but its violent suppression by the Crown was eye-opening:

> Such a conflict was anything but unusual from Diderot's point of view; it was emblematic of how religion functioned more generally in the world. Far from bringing people together, it seemed that each religious faction saw their adversaries as either spiritual infidels or political foes that needed to be crushed. Diderot later explained this phenomenon in the plainest of terms: "I have seen the deist arm himself . . . against the atheist; the deist and the atheist attack the Jew; the atheist, the deist and the Jew band together against the Christian; the Christian, the deist, the atheist, and the Jew oppose the Muslim; the atheist, the deist, the Jew, the Muslim and a multitude of Christian sects attack the Christian." (Curran)

He found alternatives to such intolerance in Epicurean philosophy, particularly Lucretius, and the skeptical theology of Spinoza, who "rejected revelation and denied the possibility that a God could exist outside the boundaries of nature and philosophy." Impiety was in the air, and Diderot breathed deeply. He befriended Rousseau in 1742, and corresponded with Voltaire, whose own education exalted science above dogma. He married a woman his father disapproved of, and while it was not a particularly happy marriage and he would take several lovers in the decades that followed, he seems to have respected his wife as a person.

Above all, Diderot was not a puritan. He enjoyed the appetites and disliked the forebodings of Pascal, who was, according to Curran, "Hobbes in a hair shirt." When Diderot published his *Philosophical Thoughts* with its restless questioning of authority, Curran says, he

> no longer had any need for Roman Catholicism and its spiteful trickster of a God. Yet the writer remained wary of the emptiness of atheism. While it may be hard to understand now, the most frightening aspect of a godless world was not godlessness itself; it was what remained after God was gone: soulless humans who seemed little more than machines living in a world that was potentially determinist, where all future events were preordained, not by an ominous deity, but by a set of mechanistic rules.

He thought bravely, but Diderot was not a martyr. When, in 1749, he was arrested for attacking morality and religion and taken to the prison at Vincennes, he denied having authored *Letter on the Blind* and *The Indiscreet Jewels*. Work on the great *Encyclopédie* was already beginning—a monumental intellectual construction that would involve dozens of authors, including Americans Benjamin Franklin and Benjamin Rush, several editors, several publishers in more than one country, delays, censorings, hatchet-jobs, betrayals, and salvations—and friends came to Diderot's aid, seeing to it that he had access to books and was not held in the worst dungeons. On his release, he threw himself into the enlightened project, subtitled "a Systematic Dictionary of the Sciences, Arts and Crafts," and worked like a mule till its completion. The eleventh volume of illustrative plates was published in 1772, the seventeenth and final volume of articles in 1766.

In our time of thick-headed leaders promoting ignorance and lies, the contemplation of an irreverent shrine to human learning is inspiring. The *Encyclopédie's* editors created a new canon of thinkers and "intellectual heroes," such as "Bacon, Leibnitz, Descartes, Locke, Newton, Buffon, Fontenelle, and Voltaire"—as listed by Andrew Curran. Diderot's collaborator, the mathematician Jean le Rond d'Alembert, promoted a modern curriculum, and "what one might call an Enlightenment version of manifest destiny." Diderot himself was pursuing dangerous free-thinking not just in individual essays, but in the way the work's system subverted society's dominant irrationality. One section subtitled "Science of God" toyed with atheism. Curran points out that

> Closer readers got the joke: the more one studies the so-called Science of God, the more it becomes clear that religion leads inevitably to occult and irrational practices. Indeed, within the *Encycplopédie's* overall breakdown of human knowledge, the so-called Science of God could just as easily have been classified under humankind's ability to "imagine" as its capacity to "reason."

Ultimately, Diderot placed religious dogma in the realm of make-believe. But he couldn't do so directly. In order to get past relentless censorship, he had to create a subterranean system of satirical connections: "After all, it was the repressive elements of the *ancien régime* that spawned the book's brilliant feints, satire, and irony, not to mention its overall methodological apparatus and structure." Curran adds, "The most famous example is the entry on 'Anthropophages' or 'Cannibals': its cross-reference directed readers to the entries for 'Altar,' 'Communion,' and 'Eucharist.'"

To me, Diderot represents humanity without idealism—or

without the totalizing idealism of Rousseau, with its attendant isolation and paranoia. Curran makes a very good case for Diderot as a champion of liberal ideas about sexuality, learning, freedom, limited monarchy, and the abolition of slavery, though these progressive principles are somewhat counterweighted by his art criticism, which could be narrow-minded, and his occasional subterfuge with women. The love of his life was a brilliant spinster, Louise-Henriette Volland, whom he called Sophie for her wisdom, and it is in letters to her that we might see Diderot's vulnerable yearnings and desires. Alas, Sophie burned many of them, and requested that her own letters be returned to her as well, "which she presumably consigned to a fireplace shortly thereafter." Their affair lasted through the trials of completing the *Encyclopédie*, including periods when it was shut down and Diderot "was in grave danger of being imprisoned." Curran quotes one of Diderot's surviving letters to her:

> I am writing without being able to see. I came. I wanted to kiss your hand and return home quickly thereafter. I will return without that gift . . . It is nine o'clock. I am writing you that I love you; I at least want to write it to you, but I don't know if the pen is bending to my will. Won't you come down so that I can tell you this, and then flee?
>
> Adieu, my Sophie, good night. Your heart must be telling you that I am here. This is the first time that I am writing in the dark. This situation should arouse loving thoughts in me. I am feeling only one; it is that I am unable to leave. The hope of seeing you for a moment is holding me back, and I continue to speak to you without knowing if I am actually forming letters. Wherever you see nothing [on this paper], read that I love you.

The author of *Letter on the Blind* writing fervently in the dark—it's a beautiful image of Diderot the man, for whom the intellectual life is never divorced from the predicament of personhood, and for whom dramatic dialogues would as a result be the most apposite form of discourse.

A man of his time, Diderot associated thinking with masculinity and thought of Sophie, in consequence, as hermaphroditic. But he was also correct in seeing sexual binaries as only part of the story—there's a bit of the hermaphrodite in all of us.

WRITING ABOUT A GENIUS from the past, one has two choices. Either we make of him an image of ourselves, taking the ideas that most suit us to buttress our own thinking, or we seek him in historical context, trying to understand his distinct identity. The example of Diderot thwarts us in both cases, it would seem, demanding the flexibility and doubt of real engagement. That's why his philosophical dialogues fascinate—they subvert the doctrinaire, while their undeniable vitality draws us in. His literary experiments, *The Nun* and *Jacques the Fatalist* (both posthumously published), provoke with their style as well as their subjects. *The Nun* deals frankly with sexuality, while *Jacques* seems a philosophical road novel. It was admired by Goethe, and its opening reads like a modern work:

> How had they met? By chance, like everybody else. What were their names? What's it to you? Where were they coming from? Does anyone really know where they're going? What were they saying? The Master wasn't saying anything, and Jacques was saying that his Captain used to say that everything that happens to us here below, for good and for ill, was written there, on high.

The few pages I've read of this novel (I hope to go further one day) reminded me of *Candide* crossed with Isaac Bashevis Singer's "Gimpel the Fool."

Such open-mindedness about identity is one of Diderot's chief attractions, and we can see it especially in another of his major dialogues, *D'Alembert's Dream*—which again fictionalizes his contemporaries in the manner of Plato. The dialogue involves a Dr. Bordeu and Mademoiselle de L'Espinasse, who has overheard D'Alembert talking in his sleep, with rushes of insight coming, it would seem, straight out of the unconscious. Curran writes,

> Bordeu—as a medical practitioner—begins his conversation by underscoring the utility of masturbation for both men and women. As he explains it, both sexes can suffer from pent-up and potentially deleterious surpluses of sexual energy. After cheerfully volunteering that sometimes one simply needs to give "nature a hand on occasion," he then moves on to the question of other nonprocreative sexual acts, including those by members of the same sex. Mademoiselle de L'Espinasse's objection that such coupling is "against nature" incites an authoritative reply from Bordeu that numbers among the boldest statements in Diderot's entire corpus: "Nothing that exists can be against nature or outside nature. . . ." Same-sex attraction and love is entirely natural, according to this principle, by dint of the simple fact that it exists.

Sexual identity is a major theme of *The Nun*, which exposes religious hypocrisy as well. *D'Alembert's Dream* considers ideas important not only to mathematics and philosophy, but also to anyone questioning notions of the self. As Richard Wilbur put it in a poem, "What is an individual thing?" Indeed. And is there a more profound question?

"Many of the stimulating ideas in *D'Alembert's Dream*," writes Curran, "have their roots in Lucretius's *De rerum natura*. This was not the first time that the *philosophe* had drawn from the Roman poet's unpredictable, vibrant, and destabilizing understanding of nature." The idea of a

> churning universe . . . gives rise to one of the most powerful moments in the *Dream*. This is when D'Alembert realizes

that the human race, too, is but a fleeting occurrence within this endless invention and reinvention of nature: "Oh, vanity of human thought! oh poverty of all our glory and labors! oh how pitiful, how limited is our vision! There is nothing real except eating, drinking, living, making love and sleeping. . . ."

If the materialism of the vision bothers you, try the translation by Ian Johnston, which is available online. You might find a sort of Darwinian consolation in nature, where everything is organically related. D'Alembert's sleep-talking outbursts are fevered poetry. Here's one of the earliest in the dialogue, in Johnston's translation:

> . . . he started to shout, "Mademoiselle de L'Espinasse! Mademoiselle de L'Espinasse!" "What do you want?" "Have you sometimes seen a swarm of bees going out of their hive? . . . The world, or the general mass of matter, is the large hive. . . . Have you seen them move out to the end of a tree branch to form a long cluster of small winged animals, all hooked to one another by their feet? . . . This cluster is a being, an individual, an animal of some sort. . . . But these clusters all have to be similar to each other. . . . Yes, if he allowed only one homogenous material. . . . Have you seen them?" "Yes, I've seen them." "Have you seen them?" "Yes, my friend, I tell you I have." "If one of these bees decides somehow to pinch the bee to which it is hanging, what do you think will happen? Tell me." "I have no idea." "Tell me, anyway. . . . So you don't know, but the philosopher knows . . . yes, he does. If you ever see him, and you're bound to see him sometime, for he promised me you would, he'll tell you that the second bee will pinch the one next to it, that in the entire cluster there would be as many sensations aroused as there are small animals, that everything will get aroused, shift itself, change position and shape, that a noise will arise, small cries, and that someone who had never seen a group like that arrange itself would be tempted

to assume it was an animal with five or six hundred heads and a thousand or twelve hundred wings. . . ."

The philosopher, like the scientist and the poet, must be an observer. Diderot rigorously adhered to this belief, and to the freedom of making his own connections. That he did so while never forgetting the suffering individual and the life of the body makes him, in my view, heroic. What others have made of him is another matter. During the French Revolution (according to legend) his lead coffin was dug up to make bullets.

2019

Neruda's Voice

I live, I still live, and I think many of us live inside the world Neruda discovered.

—ARIEL DORFMAN

. . . the voice is perhaps the most lasting incarnation of any existence. . . . It is in voices . . . that the dead continue to live.

—ALASTAIR REID

There is no insurmountable solitude. All paths lead to the same goal: to convey to others what we are.

—PABLO NERUDA

FORTY-FIVE YEARS after his death, Pablo Neruda's poetry still has the power to astonish and appall, awaken, and chill us and leave us shaking our heads in bafflement or respect. There is such breadth and profligate intelligence in the work, which ranges from opaque surrealism to big-hearted populism to Pan-American epic to shocking propaganda, that one hardly knows where to place it in our era of thwarted emotions. Clearly it is not of our time. Given Neruda's relations with women, it is certainly not of the time of #MeToo. The work will not always sit well beside a mature feminist consciousness, and, of course, it will not please ideologues who can't tell one form of socialism from another. Neruda changed, and his circumstances changed. As a man, he could be a monster of egotism and a courageous dissident, a purblind Stalinist and a Roosevelt democrat. His poetry incarnates these shifts and siftings and restless experiments. The past is a moving target. Poetry keeps it alive.

Neruda's poetry is embodied, contradictory, expressing public and private iterations of the life of a man, but we live in a time strait-jacketed by either/or thinking: either you're a womanizer or you're a flawless saint; either you're a Libertarian or you're a Stalinist; either you're with us or you're against us. Neruda frustrates contemporary appetites for correctness and justice, and some readers will dismiss him precisely on such limited grounds, as if the past could be purified to meet our astringent demands. To say Neruda was flawed is laughable. Humanity is flawed. That's what makes us *human*.

A solid new biography of Neruda by Mark Eisner frets at the issue of reception. In an epilogue, Eisner quotes a handful of Chilean university students—millennials in 2014, who sound a lot like my own students now. One of them offers, "Poetry that idealizes the feminine image, highlighting only its physical attributes from a male perspective, doesn't work as well in the twenty-first century as it did before, at least for me and my friends." It's a perfectly legitimate complaint that might help male poets find new ways of writing about erotic love—awfully hard to do without an "object." Yet the student is also choosing to overlook aspects of the past that do not conform to present views, on the authority of one generation's perspective, and I can't help feeling that, somewhere, a living baby is being thrown out with the foul old bathwater. (This "presentism" comes in a decade when the study of history on university campuses is at an all-time low.) Another student says, "Neruda seems to be loaded with a basic machismo, good bourgeois taste with the Communist flag in hand, and a pompous heroism that seems very far from us." *Very far from us.* Again, I question any education that assumes its purpose is to reify the present without trying to understand the past. A third student opines,

> In my opinion, Pablo Neruda seems an ideal example of what's happening today with the "authority figure" in diverse subjects, like politics and religion. . . . Neruda is the figure of a poet fallen from the heavens, a fallen angel, as certain truths about him have come to light and knocked him from his pedestal. . . . Neruda's consecration as a poet is not enough in our culture now; his failings as a human being must also be acknowledged.

Valid as these feelings may be, they arise from another fallacy—that admiration of a poet must perforce be consecration. Either/or. Between extremities we run our course. If Neruda was turned into a posthumous object of veneration, that is hardly the fault of his poetry. And his poetry means his voice as a human being, which his friend and translator Alastair Reid called "the most lasting legacy of any existence." We live in a time of absolutist judgments, when, as Auden put it, dead writers are "punished under a foreign code of conscience." It's inevitable, I suppose: "The words of a dead man / Are modified in the guts of the living." Yet even as we strive to hear from more diverse voices in our present day, we too often deny diversity by policing the past, trying to cleanse it of anything incorrect or unseemly. We must be able to reside with human imperfection, critical but compassionate and curious, or we will lose the diversity of art.

Justice for Pablo Neruda, and for his readers, would be to acknowledge his sins without losing sight of his accomplishment—meaning his voice. While writing this, I listened on

YouTube to Neruda's cultivated tenor declaiming lines of his masterpiece, "The Heights of Macchu Picchu," which some have called the greatest poem of the Spanish language, and I found its rhythms compelling—big breaths of chanted sound. Here are a few lines in Eisner's translation:

Rise up and be born with me, brother.

From the deepest reaches of your
disseminated sorrow, give me your hand.
You will not return from the depths of rock.
You will not return from the subterranean time.
It will not return, your hardened voice.
They will not return, your drilled eyes.
Look at me from the depths of the earth,
plowman, weaver, silent shepherd:
tender of the guardian guanacos:
mason of the impossible scaffold:
water-bearer of Andean tears:
goldsmith of crushed fingers:
farmer trembling on the seed:
potter poured out into your clay:
bring all your old buried sorrows
to the cup of this new life.

As Eisner points out, no less a purveyor of opinions than Harold Bloom "claims that Neruda 'can be regarded as Whitman's truest heir. The poet of *Canto General* is a worthier rival than any other descendant of *Leaves of Grass*.'" Bloom's narrative of heirs and anxieties is easily sniffed at, yet he accurately identifies a level of magnitude in Neruda's accomplishment. *Nerudismo*, to use a term of derision sometimes applied by Neruda's own contemporaries, can feel positively Whitmanesque: big-shouldered, open-armed. Yet Neruda as a teenager was producing gorgeous delicate love poems, and soon after that prose of hermetic surrealism, and soon after that a poetry with grand historical vision of a sort we'd be hard-pressed to find in North America. He had his phases of socialist realism, wrote a perfectly awful ode on Stalin's death, and accepted prizes from the Soviets, yet the great odes and "thing poems" of his later years are delightful. Did he contradict himself? Most certainly. Another poet I would compare him to is Yeats, both for his public life and his personal idiocies. Flawed men who wrote some great poetry—I wouldn't want to live in a world without them.

I knew Alastair Reid, the Scottish poet who superbly translated Borges and Neruda—writers of the right and the left—and loved them both as men, loved their voices. Eisner quotes from Alastair's memoir of these two men a lovely anecdote of Neruda's generosity: "Once, in Paris, while I was explaining some liberty I had taken, he stopped me and put his hand on my shoulder: 'Alastair, don't just translate my poems. I want you to improve them.'" Later, Alastair would write a very fine poem, "1973," about Neruda dying right at the moment the coup toppled Chile's first truly popular government and rolled in seventeen years of dictatorship under Pinochet. I remember that autumn. Auden died just a week after Neruda, and it seemed two giants of world poetry had been felled. I met Alastair soon after, when he came to teach at the college where I was a student, and I remember him reading another tribute, "Translator to Poet," which Eisner quotes late in his book:

There are only the words left now. They lie like tombstones
or the stone Andes where the green scrub ends.
I do not have the heart to chip away
at your long lists of joy, which alternate
their iron and velvet, all the vegetation
and whalebone of your chosen stormy coast.
So much was written hope, with every line
extending life by saying, every meeting

ending in expectation of the next.
It was your slow intoning voice which counted,
bringing a living Chile into being
where poetry was bread, where books were banquets.
Now they are silent, stony on the shelf.
I cannot read them for the thunderous silence,
the grief of Chile's dying and your own,
death being the one definitive translation.

What Alastair taught was the joyful humility of reading, allowing other presences their imperfect existences—that final translation being the limit of all our lives. Neruda's life, then, to the degree that we can know it, is instructive, even as a fading coexistence with the poems.

LITERARY BIOGRAPHY is a strange addiction. One knows it's all provisional, and one learns skepticism about any connection between the life and the work. The self is so unknowable, flickering and transient, so how can we know another? Reading a life is like reading a poem—full of ambiguity, which involves consciousness that we are *reading*. Was there ever a time when no one doubted authority? Even the great biographer Richard Holmes has said in a recent interview with Andrew Motion that "biographies take place cumulatively on the subject. There's very rarely *one* biography. They build through time. . . ." If Mark Eisner's life of Neruda sometimes feels a bit flat and declarative in style, it's still a thoughtful and valuable book, linking the meaning of Neruda's public life to the state of our world now, with versions of fascism ascendant on both the right and the left.

Like most biographies, this one begins with a blur of begats. Neruda was born Ricardo Eliecer Neftali Reyes Basoalto in southern Chile in 1904. I was jet-lagged while reading the early pages, and couldn't recount them to you if I tried. I began to wake up when the boy Neftali took the name Pablo Neruda at age sixteen, by which time he had already developed sympathies for the indigenous Mapuche people of Chile and a grasp of class differences. Prodigious in both poetry and romance, he was nineteen when he published *The Book of Twilights*, twenty when he produced a book that has now sold well over a million copies, *Twenty Love Poems and a Desperate Song.** For a while he studied French pedagogy at university in Santiago, but the distractions of literature and sex already dominated his life. The universal struggle of getting a living led him to the foreign service, and at twenty-three he was posted as Chilean consul in Rangoon, Burma (now Myanmar). Like his contemporary, Auden, he pursued an international life, much of it free of political ideology, following his own passions and proclivities. Younger than the modernists then ascendant in Europe, Neruda's generation was sympathetic to their experiments, particularly to surrealism. His international experience would eventually contribute to his global fame as a literary rock star, but in those early diplomatic years he was poor and isolated. Eisner confesses to some queasiness about Neruda's racial attitudes in Asia, particularly his treatment of local women and prostitutes. He records several encounters, versions of which appear in the poet's memoirs, one of which might have been a rape:

> Neruda's behavior, both here and throughout his time in Asia, was imperialism perpetrated on a human scale, an exact replica of the imperialism perpetrated on a geopolitical scale against which he ranted both while in Asia and while writing his memoirs. . . .
>
> His narcissism is further expressed in the way he integrates the woman's duty of cleaning his personal excrement

---

*I prefer the rhythm of W. S. Merwin's title, *Twenty Love Poems and a Song of Despair*, a slender book published with an elegant white cover, and one of the first poetry books I acquired on my own.

into the story of his violation of her. It amounts to the divinization of his excrement, as it is a sublime goddess who empties his chamber pot. The goddess merits less consideration than even a prostitute, who Neruda would at least have paid for her services.

Eisner sees Neruda's opium use and sex life in Asia as a drama of the suffering ego, the *agon* from which the early poetry was made. Surrounded by Buddhists, Neruda rejected their vision of enlightenment in favor of a more personal drama, a struggle that would eventually have its parallel in politics.

He was working on poems that would eventually comprise the three volumes of *Residence on Earth*—that marvelous visionary title—and would contain some of his most popular poems, like "Walking Around":

Comes a time I'm tired of being a man.
Comes a time I check out the tailor's or the movies
shriveled, impenetrable, like a felt swan
launched into waters of origin and ashes.

A whiff from the barber shops has me wailing.
All I want is a break from rocks and wool,
all I want is to see neither buildings nor gardens,
no shopping centers, no bifocals, no elevators.

Comes a time I'm tired of my feet and my fingernails
and my hair and my shadow.
Comes a time I'm tired of being a man.

The poem extends its list of injustices, some more trivial than others. It's a howl long before *Howl*, and indeed the Beats felt they owed a great deal to Neruda.

But his life at this point was a series of evasions, and when almost by accident he found himself consul in Batavia (now Jakarta), his precipitous marriage to Maria Antonia Hagenaar

Vogelzang, a woman unsympathetic to literature, seems part of a desperate pattern. Pablo and Maruca, as she was more affectionately known, eventually had a daughter together, Malva Marina, who suffered from hydrocephaly, and whose neglect was one of Neruda's worst actions. The girl would die at age eight, by which time Neruda and Maruca were separated. The poet's vitality was sometimes sustained by a clueless ego, and this was not the only time he turned his back on the suffering of others.

Eisner's book really comes to life when Neruda, age thirty, takes diplomatic posts in Spain, developing his connection to Spanish writers like Federico García Lorca, deepening his relationship to Chile's mother country. In Spain, Neruda developed his theory of "A poetry impure as old clothes, as a body, with its food stains and shame, with wrinkles, observations, dream, vigilance, prophecies, declarations of love and hate, beasts, blows, idylls, manifestos, denials, doubts, affirmations, taxes." As civil war erupted in 1936, Neruda took on a heroic stature that was not a pose. The stakes were real and vital, and he was one of the poets who could see them clearly. Like Auden, Orwell, and Hemingway, he witnessed history being made, but as a diplomat he had additional responsibility for the people involved, and he acquitted himself well. Poems like "I Explain Some Things" brought stark reportage of events into literature:

> You will ask why his poetry
> doesn't speak to us of dreams, of the leaves,
> of the great volcanoes of his native land?
>
> Come and see the blood in the streets,
> come and see
> the blood in the streets,
> come and see the blood
> in the streets!

In 1936 García Lorca's execution by fascists affected Neruda profoundly:

Lorca's fate moved the poets to become active participants in the war, not just observers. Pablo Neruda had become a different poet; now he became a different man. There were no more surrealist dead doves or pumpkins listening. There was the blood of children. There was Lorca's blood, and much more to follow.

Neruda and his new partner, Delia del Carril, escaped first to France, then to Chile, where he worked valiantly to resettle Spanish refugees. To make his love life possible he was acting the cad toward Maruca, but in politics he was genuinely intrepid. He didn't see the Stalinist takeover of the Spanish left as a danger the way Orwell did, largely because he focused on the suffering of the Spanish people and tried to do something about it. His blindness to Stalin's crimes would blight his biography, to be sure, but in the 1940s he was more a compassionate politician than an ideologue.

Neruda set himself in opposition to the conservative government of his homeland, formally joining the Communist Party in 1945. In hindsight, of course, this seems a blunder, but Eisner makes a good case that Neruda saw communism as the only viable way to oppose the economic and political corruption of his country. In 1947, now a senator, he addressed the Chilean senate in defense of an article he had published on the "Crisis of Democracy." Here again his ideas do not seem Stalinist, but responsible criticisms of an untenable status quo. He quoted Franklin Delano Roosevelt's four freedoms—as succinct a formula for a just society as any I know: ". . . freedom of speech and expression; freedom of every person to worship God in his own way; freedom from want; freedom from fear."

This public stance was not easy. In an intolerant state, he was putting his life in danger, and he was not unafraid of the prospect of incarceration and worse. When the state issued a warrant for his arrest, Neruda went into hiding, protected by literary friends and fellow communists. This is another of the best chapters in Eisner's book, recounting Neruda's escape over the Andes to Argentina.* His fame made him into a Robin Hood figure, supported by the very people who were the subjects of his poems. He spoke of these trials in his Nobel lecture in 1971, relating a beautiful story of aid received from mountain peasants:

> And I remember vividly: when we wanted to give the people of the mountain a few coins for their songs, their food, the water, the beds, and the roof over our heads—the unexpected shelter we had found—they refused our offering without even a gesture. They had done what they could for us, and nothing more. And in that silent "nothing more," many things were understood; perhaps acknowledgement, perhaps dreams themselves.

Always seeking connection, Neruda links the politics of the time and the lives of "ordinary people," whatever we take such a phrase to mean, with the imaginative work of the poet. In this he seems Emersonian, a representative man.

Yet there remain just as many stories of Neruda as the "Champagne Communist" whose devotion to pleasure proved constantly distracting. He was in many ways a coward with women, hiding from Delia his love for the woman who would become his third wife, Matilde Urrutia, and eventually hiding from Matilde his affair with her niece. If you want your poets to be saints, don't look to Neruda. He went into public exile, living in Europe, visiting the Soviet Union.† He was

---

*The 2016 movie, *Neruda*, presents an unsentimental version of this tale.

†*Il Postino*, a book, movie, and even an opera, dramatizes this period in his life.

mobbed by fans at airports and in restaurants. He got fat. His political poems were more strident and sentimental, though in 1963 he finally managed to denounce Communist totalitarianism. Decades of silence about Stalin's crimes, years in which he turned his back on friends who suffered under Stalin, could hardly be assuaged by these changes of heart. Neruda even slandered his friend Czesław Miłosz, who had left Poland for France, "in an article entitled 'The Man Who Ran Away,' naming Miłosz . . . 'an agent of American imperialism.'" Years later, Neruda remained incapable of understanding what he had done:

> A decade and a half after Neruda wrote his denunciation of his former friend, the two saw each other at the 1966 PEN Conference in New York. Neruda saw Miłosz across the room, cried, "Czesław!" and rushed to embrace him. Miłosz turned his face away and Neruda said, "But, Czesław, that was politics." (Eisner)

On YouTube you can find films of the corpulent, dignified Neruda from these years, and see in him both gravitas and clownishness, a face easy to caricature, giving him an aspect of the Chaplinesque. He's one of the instantly recognizable figures of modern art, like another Pablo, his good friend Picasso, who had also worked through multiple phases of creativity and danced awkwardly with Stalinism. Genius is no proof of wisdom.

We are left with Neruda's death from prostate cancer, and for a time the death of Chile, the latter partly orchestrated by the CIA. If Neruda's death was brought about in the same way, the evidence has not yet been produced, despite many attempts to make it so. Eisner reports that new genetic tests on Neruda's exhumed bones may yet have another story to tell. Or may not.

And we are left with Neruda's voice. Watch his dignified manner in interviews with the likes of Gabriel García

Márquez, or listen to him reciting "The Heights of Macchu Picchu," or consider Eisner's account of a reading Neruda gave at the Royal Festival Hall in London in April 1972 with his friend Alastair Reid:

Reid read the English first, followed by Neruda reading the Spanish, in sections, so that the "sense comes first and the sound follows," as Reid put it. If four decades earlier Neruda's voice had been nasal and monotone, now it resounded, especially pronounced by the crisscross rhythm between the Spanish and the English, alternating long strands or stanzas or just couplets back and forth, the poems broken up as if into meter, creating varying speeds and tension and song. Reid had heard Neruda read many times, but on that night he sensed something truly special: the Chilean's voice was "spreading itself like a balm over the English audience." It was "a magical sound."

2018

The Perils of Fame

SYLVIA PLATH AND SEAMUS HEANEY

They are killing her again.

—FRIEDA HUGHES

Don't you see—fame will ruin everything.

—TED HUGHES, QUOTING SYLVIA PLATH

So this is what an afterlife can come to?

—SEAMUS HEANEY

ONE OF OUR most powerful stories is that of the misread person, judged and condemned by everyone, ultimately unseen. We make these narratives worse with our ridiculous social media, the lack of circumspection as persons and reputations go crashing down in the flames of righteousness and vindictive gossip. How little justice really results from our cries for justice, our certitude, our raging egos, our "likes"; how much could, in a better world, remain open to nuance, ambiguity, and doubt. How little mercy we show each other, how little forgiveness. But social media only amplifies human tendencies that have always been with us, wherever two or more are gathered in the name of anything.

Consider the problem of fame, one of the most universal human desires and one of the most disastrous, how it underlies literary ambition, the "fair guerdon" praised by Milton. Consider also the paradox that literature requires solitude, not only for its composition but for access to the deeper waters of inspiration, beyond ego and its siren calls. Writers thrash in the arms of this paradox, wanting to say something that will speak to future generations, wanting the opportunities that fame affords without being destroyed by the judgments that follow it. The position is impossible.

One could argue that Sylvia Plath was destroyed by fame even before she became famous, though her most enduring fame was achieved after she committed suicide on February 11, 1963. She became famous not for herself, not even for the fierce, exacting beauty of her best poems, but as a figure easily misread by what she had called "The peanut-crunching crowd"—a martyr, an icon for feminists, a cautionary tale, a bitch-goddess. None of these judgments have touched the reality of her person or the reasons her poetry stands out in comparison to the writing of others.

Plath was not a poet of suicide any more than Homer was a poet of sailing. She was smart, ambitious, hugely talented, disciplined, complicated. She suffered from depression, but depression did not define every day of her life. She was every bit as much a mystery as you and I, untouchable by the facts of her life, no matter who mines and exhibits them. Anne Stevenson's 1989 biography, *Bitter Fame*, excelled because it was written by a poet of Plath's stature and generation, but it was probably compromised by Plath's sister-in-law, Olwyn Hughes, who did not know her well and wanted to defend the reputation of her brother, Ted. The massive new biography by Heather Clark, *Red Comet*, represents a fuller picture, more thorough research, and freedom to quote from papers unavailable to earlier writers, but does it get any closer to the "truth" about Sylvia Plath? I doubt it. Clark's laudable program is to rescue Plath from the critical residue of the past sixty years—the misrepresentations, judgments, opinions, assumptions, misreadings. On the whole, she succeeds in making us care, if we had not already cared, about Plath's brilliance and its place in the world. But one must still be cautious when reading the poems in this biographical light. Like all the best poetry, like life itself, Plath's poems cannot be fully or conveniently explained as phenomena.

In 2004, Plath's daughter, the artist and poet Frieda Hughes, collaborated on a "Restored Edition" of her mother's most famous book, *Ariel*, and wrote in her measured foreword,

> Since she died, my mother has been dissected, analyzed, reinterpreted, reinvented, fictionalized, and in some cases completely fabricated. It comes down to this: Her own words describe her best, her ever-changing moods defining the way she viewed her world and the manner in which she pinned down her subjects with a merciless eye.

But why do we want to think we know the person who wrote the poems? What is it that sends us probing for certainty we cannot have?

Ted Hughes edited the *Ariel* manuscript after Plath's death and published two different versions in England and America. It became a bestseller and one of the most influential poetry books of the century. Hughes had removed some poems, added others left on Plath's desk, like the much-anthologized "Edge," which is often read as a sort of suicide note. He said he wanted to make it the best book he could, and of course the peanut-crunching crowd still second-guesses his motives. Whatever one thinks of individual poems, the book made by Ted Hughes gives Plath's suicide greater prominence, while Plath's own manuscript couches her most nightmarish poems in a broader, more life-affirming narrative. As Frieda Hughes put it, "My mother described her *Ariel* manuscript as beginning with the word 'Love' and ending with the word 'Spring.'"

As a lyric poet of genuine magnitude, Plath is often compared to Emily Dickinson—a major writer by any measure and also, to some extent, a mystery. Like Dickinson, she is not everyone's idea of a genius. But re-reading her poems, trying to see them freshly, trying to do them justice, one can be amazed by her technical prowess, her daring, her conceptual leaps, even while flinching at some of her more controversial choices. Read her bee poems again, or "The Moon and the Yew Tree" or "Poppies in October," which ends, "O my God, what am I / That these late mouths should cry open / In a forest of frost, in a dawn of cornflowers!" Louise Glück's flower poems contributed to her winning the Nobel Prize, but she has had a longer life than Plath, with time to develop and change. One can't help wondering what more Sylvia Plath might have accomplished as both novelist and poet had not events—which we do not really understand even now—led to her death on that dark cold morning in London.

SETTING THE SHORT LIFE and "blazing art" of Sylvia Plath beside the work of a more fortunate poet, in some ways the luckiest of all poets, Seamus Heaney, may at first seem very strange. But as different as these two writers were, they were both caught in the webs of fame. Plath, born in 1932, was an American who fashioned a mid-Atlantic voice. Heaney, born seven years later, began very much within a local habitation in Ulster, eventually becoming a beloved international figure. Her life was unlucky, his the opposite. Heaney maintained a close friendship with Ted Hughes, who was called by many a kind and considerate man, by others a monster and destroyer, even a murderer. I doubt Plath ever read a poem by Heaney, but he read and wrote perceptively about hers. Another connection between them came via their mutual friend Robert Lowell, and is more difficult to pin down, a probing quality in voice and phrasing, the very material of their distinct voices. Plath's early poem called "Letter to a Purist" might have appealed to Heaney, who also felt affection for the impure, the guttural, the earthbound. Here is Plath:

O my great idiot, who
With one foot
Caught (as it were) in the muck-trap
Of skin and bone,
Dithers with the other way out
In the preposterous provinces of the madcap
Cloud-Cuckoo,
Agawp at the impeccable moon.

Her stance is affectionate, intelligent, her phrasing as impeccable as that moon. The tug between heaven and earth exists in a lot of poetry, beautifully irreconcilable. Heaney feels it more plainly in "The Guttural Muse":

A girl in a white dress
Was being courted out among the cars:
As her voice swarmed and puddled into laughs
I felt like some old pike all badged with sores
Wanting to swim in touch with soft-mouthed life.

Plath's most famous and controversial poems—"Daddy," "Lady Lazarus," "Edge"—have a confronting audacity and attack that Heaney never aspired to, even in poems dealing with Ireland's tribal violence. Heaney's poetry is genial and what we call "sane," easier to love. Plath has often been victimized by profound misogyny, something which she rightly sensed in her own lifetime and which has never really disappeared. Heaney has the usual male prerogative, an entrée to the world of politics that Plath more often touched in her fiction. His career was fostered, and so was hers—not just by Ted

Hughes, but also by countless editors and friends. He lived to the age of 74, she died at 30, and one wishes both had lived longer. The difference hurts.

ANOTHER REASON I compare these two poets is that I've just read the new books about them. Heather Clark's biography is authoritative and huge—more than nine hundred pages on a short life. Cutting a hundred pages of redundant details would not have hurt. I remain unconvinced that every high school date or term paper needs to be taken as a key to her story. But the biography's final two hundred pages compel attention, and the final sentence (which I'll get to later) might be the single most beautiful thing ever said about Sylvia Plath.

R. F. Foster's slender book *On Seamus Heaney*, published in Princeton University Press's Writers on Writers series, comes to just over two hundred pages and is one of the most elegant works of criticism I have ever read. Foster, a historian who published a superb two-volume life of W. B. Yeats, has paid tribute to Heaney by the care with which he shapes his brief study. His little book, like Clark's gargantuan one, intends at least partly a defense of the poet against his detractors. Heaney might have been easier to love, less troubled, luckier, but we would not care about him if he had not, like Plath, made the most of his gifts in the time he was given.

Both Plath and Heaney admired Yeats, a poet who could do almost anything, who forged a position both public and private in verse of uncompromising authority. Plath died in a house where Yeats had once lived. Heaney lived just a year longer than Yeats and, as an Irish poet, albeit a Catholic Ulster one, could not have ignored the heights of his forebear's accomplishment. Such ambitions imply the strongest regard for and faith in literature, its potential for global efficacy no matter how humble its origins.

When I first read Plath as an undergraduate in the 1970s, she was already set aside by judgment, either the misogyny dismissing her as a madwoman, calling her poems hysterical, or the feminism that made a martyr of her. She could not really be read "on her own merits," if that is ever possible. At that time, Heaney was unknown to most American readers. I found his work on my own and felt as if the poet were speaking on my behalf. How many millions of women have by now felt the same about Plath?

When I taught in Ireland in the 1990s, it was already fashionable in some quarters to dismiss Heaney as overrated. In *Stepping Stones* (2008), his marvelous interviews with Dennis O'Driscoll, Heaney quoted a clerihew by the critic Edna Longley, no doubt teasing her husband Michael:

Michael Longley
Is inclined to feel strongly
About being less famous
Than Seamus.

If the literary London of Plath's final years was a pressure cooker of gossip and judgment, so was Ireland for much of Heaney's career. The problem of early fame is that you have to develop in the public eye. Perhaps Plath was lucky not to have seen the figure she became—it might have curdled her ambition or driven her to some other hell of ego. Heaney lived with steadily increasing fame that soaked up much of his life, and he did so with admirable grace, never betraying his vocation even in the face of Ireland's real political turmoil. Foster notes his "charisma, style, and accessibility," his poetry's "unique ability to speak to a wide readership while retaining its own independent mysteries."

If Heaney had died at thirty, he would have been the author of two slender collections, *Death of a Naturalist* (1966) and *Door into the Dark* (1969). These comprise an admirable beginning and include seminal poems like "Digging," "Follower," "Mid-term Break," "Personal Helicon," and "Requiem for the Croppies," work in which we can see his subtle blending of politics, autobiography, and the Eros of embodied life. Foster and others have suggested that Heaney's first four books form a single stage in his development, culminating in the archeological excavations exposing tribal violence, the bog as memory, in *Wintering Out* (1972) and especially *North* (1975). "The frisson of reading *North* in 1975," Foster writes, "was unforgettable: a chill, and a recognition." It was the same for me in far northwest America. My bookish knowledge of Irish politics was insufficient, but I could already sense the importance of this poetry, somehow very much of its time and place, wary and unsentimental, but written in a way that allowed me into the experience. And there was Heaney's running commentary on the position of the poet in our time:

> How did I end up like this?
> I often think of my friends'
> Beautiful prismatic counselling
> And the anvil brains of some who hate me
>
> As I sit weighing and weighing
> My responsible *tristia*.
> For what? For the ear? For the people?
> For what is said behind-backs?

Foster knows the unspoken tensions Heaney had to negotiate, the jealousies, rivalries, and chastenings. Steering a sane course through such societal demands took immense reserves of tact.

Heaney would have been an important poet if it all ended there, but he went on to publish *Field Work, Station Island, The Haw Lantern, Seeing Things, The Sprit Level, Electric Light* (which Foster finds thin), *District and Circle,* and *Human Chain.* These books, plus his versions of Greek drama, his *Beowulf,* his fine selected poems, *Opened Ground,* and his essays, put him on a global stage, where he moved with "benign authority," as Foster puts it.

He was, as he himself once wrote uneasily, "steeped in luck"—a rare condition in a great artist. But a poet's life—as Yeats famously said—is necessarily an experiment in living, and the river-like course of Heaney's work was sustained against competing events and pressures in his own life and, above all, against an era of exceptional violence, brutality, and nihilism in his own country.

In his essay "Joy or Night: Last Things in the Poetry of W.B. Yeats and Philip Larkin," originally delivered as a lecture, Heaney averred that "when a poem rhymes, when a form generates itself, when a metre provokes consciousness into new postures, it is already on the side of life." One finds in Heaney a sustaining narrative, despite his being fully aware of the worst that humans do. His work is very much on the side of life. Was Plath on the side of death? I don't think so, and not only because of the way she structured her final book of poems. She made them, worked them, intended them to have the best life she could possibly give them. She was publishing regularly in the best magazines in the English-speaking world and had the attention of publishers and important critics like A. Alvarez, who would become one of her strongest champions. For a writer at her stage of development, she was already pretty famous, and she fought to make it so. As a woman artist, frequently prevailed upon to play the angel of the house, she experienced the profound frustrations of many women artists, her life sopped up with the needs of others, especially her children and her husband, who was himself experiencing a not-uncommon desire for freedom and escape. But she was productive, she was in every sense big with life. She was even, apparently, a better gardener than Ted. She desired the traditional roles given to women—sexual object and care-taker—

and she railed against them in fury. Her position was not at all unusual for women in her time, and perhaps also in ours. She was judged as an angry woman, but her anger in the circumstances was a form of sanity.

A LOT OF SADNESS surrounds the life and death of Sylvia Plath. What caused her depression? As Clark and others have noted, some of it might have been hereditary. But the pressures placed upon her as a student at Smith College, her own frantic desire to be the star student, the great writer, and to win a husband at all costs, certainly took their toll. Worse still was a mismanaged course of electroshock treatment under the direction of a clueless male psychiatrist. When she vanished, Clark writes, "more than two hundred and fifty newspaper articles covered the search for the missing Smith beauty." She was eventually found in her own mother's basement, having swallowed pills. But attempted suicide wasn't a regular occurrence with her, as it seems to have been with Anne Sexton, nor was she subject to the kind of mania that sent Robert Lowell into paroxysms of praise for Hitler. When she writes about that suicide attempt, or a version of it, in *The Bell Jar*, it is with an artist's detachment, including a powerful critique of the society in which she was raised.

Plath's mother, Aurelia, gets a lot of blame for Sylvia's troubles, exacerbated by the way she is portrayed in the novel. Aurelia was devastated when Ted Hughes decided to publish *The Bell Jar* in the US. It had been a modest success in England, but the suicide made it more marketable, and he wanted to establish an income for their two children. Clark's book is careful not to assign blame too easily in any of this. Aurelia was a loving mother who sacrificed a lot for her children, Aurelia was a demon of expectations—all of it is possible, and ultimately she comes across as a fine, intelligent, sad human being. Ted stated that his infidelity (with multiple women) was a kind of madness, and intimated that he and Sylvia might have reconciled.

There were other contributing factors to her final "successful" suicide. Her overtures to other men, including Alvarez, were rebuffed, she and the children were often sick during the coldest winter of the century. She was taking a crazy cocktail of medicines, some for colds, some for depression, partly prescribed by a well-meaning doctor who did not know her entire history: ". . . by early February, Plath was taking two amphetamines . . . , one opioid (codeine), one barbiturate (Drinamyl), as well as an unknown medicine for her respiratory illness. The interactions of these drugs alone could have significantly worsened her depression and anxiety. . . ." There was also the terror over her final weekend that she would be hospitalized again, including the specter of more electroshock treatment. Ted would blame everything, including himself, later writing to Anne Stevenson, "Her death was the remotest fluke, an unbelievably freakish sequence of unlucky coincidences."

Did Plath intend to die? Did she wish to be rescued? Was her final act one of revenge or despair or love? There is evidence for all of it, and Clark recounts the facts and opinions in apt detail. One of many telling anecdotes occurs toward the end of her book:

> Anthony Thwaite, Louis MacNeice and some other men were having a drink at a pub near the BBC Broadcasting House when Douglas Cleverdon walked in, "enormously shaken," and told them about Plath's death. One of the men at the table made an appalling remark ("women poets, what do you expect?"). MacNeice "rounded on the man" and told him to shut up. Thwaite felt "colossal shock" that this "quick," "capable, social" person he had grown to know through her BBC work had committed suicide.

The death would receive notice at first only in a small parish newspaper, but a week later Alvarez published a tribute in *The Observer*, and as Plath's work continued to appear in the magazines, with a large spread of poems the following summer in *The New Yorker* and the publication of *Ariel* in 1965, her fame grew and caught the second wave of feminism and surpassed it into the realm of myth. Ted Hughes endured not only the blame for her death, but the suicide of his lover, Assia Wevill, who took their daughter Shura as well. Was he guilty? Was he a monster of ego and rough sex? Was he a kind and loving father as well as a poet trying to keep faith with his art? We don't really know, do we? Perhaps the saddest fact of all for this family is that Ted and Sylvia's son, Nick, who grew up to become a marine biologist in Alaska, killed himself in 2009.

Somewhere between Anne Stevenson's title, *Bitter Fame*, and Heather Clark's *Red Comet*, we have the narratives of Sylvia Plath, best read not only as a cautionary tale but as a lesson in critical circumspection. Set those narratives aside as best you can when you read the work, including *Three Women*, her longish poem for voices that was broadcast on the BBC and is full of gorgeous passages:

> The streets may turn to paper suddenly, but I recover
> From the long fall, and find myself in bed,
> Safe on the mattress, hands braced, as for a fall.
> I find myself again. I am no shadow
> Though there is a shadow starting from my feet. I am a wife.
> The city waits and aches. The little grasses
> Crack through stone, and they are green with life.

Poets meet in the strangest places. Next to this fragment of Plath's beauty I will put a piece of Heaney's, from his poem "At the Wellhead":

> Your songs, when you sing them with your two eyes closed
> As you always do, are like a local road
> We've known every turn of in the past—
> That midge-veiled, high-hedged side-road where you stood

Looking and listening until a car
Would come and go and leave you lonelier
Than you had been to begin with. So, sing on,
Dear shut-eyed one, dear far-voiced veteran,

Sing yourself to where the singing comes from. . . .

He's not talking about Plath, of course, but that doesn't matter. I promised to mention Heather Clark's final sentence. If you don't want to know it, stop reading now. The sentence is: "Let us not desert her." It moves me right down to the ground to consider this, and all the ways people have tried to honor both her life and her work. The honor paid to their subjects by these two books about important poets deserves honor in return.

2021

Homage to Tom Stoppard

Man is in love and loves what vanishes,
What more is there to say?

—W. B. YEATS

IF YOU'RE GOING TO enthuse about a writer, it helps if that writer is a genius. Tom Stoppard fits the bill. "Every atom is a cathedral," he once wrote. I can't help feeling the same about his brain. In plays for stage, radio, and television, he has been an architect of vision and entertainment from the start, finding the poetry in science, inspired goofiness, and the grief of history. And now he has chosen the ideal biographer in Hermione Lee. *Tom Stoppard: A Life* might be premature, since Stoppard is alive and writing at nearly eighty-four, but the book is shrewdly judged and (aside from a few redundant details) well-written, with the gossip of a celebrity biography and sympathy for what a life's work really means. Professor Lee has written books on Elizabeth Bowen, Philip Roth, Willa Cather, Virginia Woolf, and Penelope Fitzgerald. Stoppard is her only living subject, and she muses on the problem of summing him up, the very predicament of her genre:

You try to bring the person to life as fully as you can on your page, your stage of written words. But in the end, this person, Tom Stoppard, will vanish into the darkness, and all those things that made this person who he was will vanish with him. He will live on in his work: you will find him there, as he has always wanted you to. Once he vanishes, he becomes his admirers. His life turns into the work he has left behind, and into other people's stories, legends, anecdotes and versions of him—of which this book is one. What I have tried to capture will only ever be one aspect of him. The relation of the written to the lived life can only be partial.

The biographer's modesty is becoming, but her book presents a commanding case for Stoppard's greatness as a man and an artist. The book is long but not too long, elegantly shaped and verbally astute, even at times poetic in its evocations of theater's evanescence. And such evanescence is Stoppard's very subject, making the glimmer of life beautiful even as it disappears. He believes a play is an event, proves it by his tireless revision during rehearsal. Even the published versions of his scripts are considered provisional, nearly as fleeting as an actor's delivery.

Stoppard emerges in this book not only as a good man but as a person interested in goodness yet undeceived about human folly. Lee only briefly allows for perceived flaws in his character: "One grand old woman of the world, an old friend of his, said to me: 'Beware of the charm.' A theatre director noted that he used his politeness to get what he wanted from people. . . . Another described him as completely, icily alone, a solitary." In short, a man of some reserve, an artist who has had to pursue his art among other people even when his personal inclinations are to remain private. But it's what he has given us in spite of everything that matters, Lee concludes: "A famous writer, who loves him dearly, said: 'He is one of the most important people in the world.'"

Lee offers superb readings of Stoppard's many works with stories of how they came into being and the talented personalities involved in mounting any play—these amount to a Who's Who of modern theater, actors, directors, moneymen, technicians. Even people who have never seen a play might have enjoyed the movie roles he has created for the likes of Sean Connery, Michelle Pfeiffer, and Gwyneth Paltrow—Stoppard has made a good living as a Hollywood script doctor and author of screenplays like *Brazil, Empire of the Sun, The Russia House,* and *Shakespeare in Love.* Lee reads his writings for television and radio as seriously as the rest. But it's in the works for the stage, from *Rosencrantz and Guildenstern Are Dead* (1966) to *Leopoldstadt* (2020), that he has built his true cathedral out of air, thin air. Well, not really out of air, but out of the language and much of the literature, science, and history it carries. Hermione Lee appears to know her subject right down to his bones, but does not overburden the book with psychological speculation beyond essential facts. Her sympathies extend to the primal wound it has taken Stoppard much of a lifetime to discover, the disappearance of his own Jewish family in the Holocaust, a truth he learned only in his fifties.

If science provides Stoppard some of his most intriguing metaphors, history and art deepen his sensibility and enlarge his range. But all of these subjects are concerned with that evanescence, memory and experience and the meaning of time, those human vanishings.

I REMEMBER WANDERING through Brno, in the Czech Republic, in 1997, and seeing a street violinist performing in front of a building pockmarked with bullet holes. Even the cemeteries appeared to have been battlefields. It was not a place that history had been kind to, and it was where Tom Stoppard's father, Eugen Sträussler, grew up. Tom was born Tomás, nearby in Zlín, hometown of his mother, Marta.

Hermione Lee's biography never gets bogged down in begats,

but runs succinctly through Stoppard's birth in 1937 and his childhood in India and England as, in his words, a "bounced Czech." There is grief inside the joke. Hitler's invasion had sent the family into exile in Singapore, cut off from any news about their home.

While Eugen and Marta were together in Singapore, Eugen's parents, Julius and Hildegard Sträussler, both in their sixties, were evicted from their house in Brno and, early in 1941, were put on the transport of Moravian Jews to the Theresienstadt concentration camp at Terezin. On 9 January 1942, a month before their son Eugen's death, they were transported to the ghetto in Riga, Latvia, where they died. . . . In 1944, Marta's parents, Rudolf Beck, aged seventy, and Regina, a chronic invalid at sixty-nine, died at Auschwitz. So did two of her four sisters, Wilma and Berta.

Stoppard was four years old when the Japanese attack on Singapore forced his family to flee again, this time, by chance, to India. His father was to follow but died in Singapore, perhaps in one of the many sunken ships or strafed from the air. After five years in Darjeeling, the widowed Marta married an Englishman, Major Kenneth Stoppard. Tom and his brother, Peter, "came to see their stepfather as a bitter, disappointed man, bigoted, xenophobic and anti-Semitic." Marta avoided all mention of their Jewish heritage, and the boys were raised in an England that might itself have been a theatrical set, complete with cricket pitches and schoolboy uniforms. Stoppard felt entirely English and loved what England seemed to stand for: reason and right in a world of warring maniacs.

Stoppard is also among the many great writers who never received a university degree. He left school at seventeen, earning his living on Grub Street until his first successes as a playwright. Working at first for newspapers in Bristol, he befriended Peter O'Toole, who was making his name as an actor at the Bristol Old Vic. The two became drinking buddies and fellow cricket buffs. Eventually, Stoppard would play on Harold Pinter's cricket team. His early years as a reporter, combined with the love of sport (he has fished with Ted Hughes), gave him a highly-developed awareness of real world troubles and a healthy sense of fun. He's the autodidact's autodidact. When he stumbled into entertainment criticism, reviewing movies as well as plays, he learned about dramatic structure and how to make a line "land" on an audience—his chief aesthetic criterion.

I was a Pinter fan before a Stoppard one. Like many people, I at first found the younger playwright's work merely clever, but in my wise old age I've seen the error. His breakthrough play, *Rosencrantz and Guildenstern Are Dead*, is not merely an exercise in absurdist clown-show theatrics, but a tragicomedy of real power. The theme of chance underlies the grim fact that his two protagonists, minor players in *Hamlet*, are soon to be disappeared. One is tempted to link these vanishings to that of Stoppard's own father, but Lee's biography generally avoids needless psychologizing. She quotes an interview in which he said, "When you take away everything plays think they're about, what's left is what all plays—all stories—are really about, and what they're really about is time. Events, things happening—Ophelia drowns! Camille coughs! Somebody has bought the Cherry Orchard!—are different manifestations of what governs the narrative we make up, just as it governs the narrative we live in: the unceasing ticktock of the universe." All the intellectual curiosity, the way he has of putting physics and mathematics comprehensibly onstage, belies what Auden called "a simple enormous grief." Or, as Yeats put it, "Man is in love and loves what vanishes." Now you see it, now you don't.

If there's an over-arching political argument to Stoppard's life's work, it is in opposition to the world's destroyers, in celebration of the makers, thinkers, and lovers with all their flaws. Late in *The Coast of Utopia*, Stoppard's 2002 trilogy of plays about nineteenth-century Russian intelligentsia, Alexander Herzen, whose idealism has been tempered by experience, argues, "History has no purpose! History knocks at a thousand gates at every moment, and the gatekeeper is chance. It takes wit and courage to make our way while our way is making us, with no consolation to count on but art and the summer lightning of personal happiness." He says this to his friends Karl Marx and Ivan Turgenev, who "ignore him and stroll away." Stoppard's politics are consistently skeptical of idealism, to put it mildly. Herzen concludes as follows:

> To go on, and to know there is no landfall on the paradisal shore, and still to go on. To open men's eyes and not tear them out. To bring what's good along with them. The people won't forgive when the future custodian of a broken statue, a stripped wall, a desecrated grave, tells everyone who passes by, "Yes—yes, all this was destroyed by the revolution." The destroyers wear nihilism like a cockade—they think they destroy because they're radicals. But they destroy because they're disappointed conservatives—let down by the ancient dream of a perfect society where circles are squared and conflict is cancelled out. But there is no such place and Utopia is its name. So until we stop killing our way towards it, we won't be grown up as human beings. Our meaning is in how we live in an imperfect world, in our time. We have no other.

He is, of course, speaking directly to us, whether or not the drama's fourth wall is broken. Ideologues of Left and Right should heed such words, but they will not because they are ideologues. We've had enough of them.

THE NEW BIOGRAPHY provides a very good introduction to the plays, but Lee knows there is no substitute for reading the scripts or seeing them performed. Again and again, I'm struck by how often vanishings occur: the premature death of Thomasina and the madness of Septimus in *Arcadia* (1993); the suicide of Konstantin in Chekhov's *The Seagull* (1997), one of Stoppard's many translations; the death by cancer of Eleanor in *Rock 'n' Roll* (2006); the way the Holocaust has diminished the cast by the end of *Leopoldstadt*. His script for the Oscar-winning *Shakespeare in Love* (1996) ends with "tears and a journey." The film is less about Shakespeare than it is about the near-miraculous anarchy of theater, the pleasures of performance. Historical inaccuracies in the movie infuriate some scholars but are part of the fun, just as Stoppard's portrayals of academics in such works as *Professional Foul* (1977, for BBC television), *Arcadia*, and *Rock 'n' Roll* prove both satirical and oddly affectionate. He puts his faith in art into Belinksy's delightful ravings about Russian literature in *Utopia*, the resonant Sappho scholarship in *Rock 'n' Roll*, and Henry's great cricket speech from *The Real Thing* (1982). Like Stoppard, Henry is a playwright of definite aesthetic beliefs who also loves the sport because, like writing, it requires precision of performance. A cricket bat is a thing made to functional specifications, which are themselves a kind of art. "It isn't better because someone says it's better," Henry says, "or because there's a conspiracy by the MCC to keep cudgels out of Lords. It's better because it's better." Stoppard and his protagonist would sympathize with Auden, who wrote, "Every high C accurately struck demolishes the theory that we are irresponsible puppets of fate or chance." Henry's aesthetic faith sets him against the political art of the Scottish nationalist, Brodie, yet Stoppard leaves room for both points of view. He doesn't have to resolve the divide between politics and art because he's writing drama, and he writes every point of view with conviction. When Henry says, "I don't think writers are sacred, but words are," he wins me over entirely, even when I can see that nobody's motives in the play are pure.

Like all great drama, Stoppard's plays hold a mirror (sometimes a funhouse mirror) up to the human situation. "We act on scraps of information," says Guildenstern before his disappearance, "sifting half-remembered directions that we can hardly separate from instinct." If quantum physics and chaos theory guide such plays as *Hapgood* (1988) and *Arcadia*, it's partly because Stoppard loved the voices of people like Richard Feynman who wrote beautifully about science. His modern character, Valentine, in *Arcadia*, a play that juxtaposes two different historical periods and sets them dancing together, says, "It's the best possible time to be alive, when almost everything you thought you knew is wrong." Stoppard's ideas are animated by the people who express them as part of their temperament.

"Dramatists become essayists at their peril," he wrote in the introduction to *Rock 'n' Roll*, his play about the life he might have led if he had remained in Czechoslovakia. The dissident Jan, who has lived on both sides of the Iron Curtain, says in Act One, "Heroic acts don't spring from your beliefs. . . . They spring from your character." Jan's friend and teacher, Max, is an aging academic who clings to his Marxist ideals but never really acts upon them. Their friendship survives political betrayal, rather like the friendship of the two men in Athol Fugard's *A Lesson from Aloes*. Fugard made his moving drama from only three characters, while Stoppard populates his plays, making a more complicated vocal music, which invites chaos even as it finds equipoise. Character matters. Max's dying wife, Eleanor, becomes one of the most moving and powerful figures in all of Stoppard because of her own acute vision. A classicist who understands that human nature has never really changed, she is outraged by her husband's dialectical materialism, which he stubbornly sees as a kind of integrity:

ELEANOR They've cut, cauterized and zapped away my breasts, my ovaries, my womb, half my bowel, and a nutmeg out of my brain, and I'm undiminished, I'm exactly who I've always been. *I am not my body.* My body is nothing without me, that's the truth of it.
She tears open her dress.

Look at it, what's left of it. It does classics. It does half-arsed feminism, it does love, desire, jealousy and fear—Christ, does it do fear!—so who's the me who's still in one piece?

MAX I know that—I know your mind is everything.

ELEANOR (*furious*) Don't you dare, Max—don't you dare reclaim that word *now*. I don't want your 'mind' which you can make out of beer cans. Don't bring it to my funeral. I want your grieving soul or nothing. I do not want your amazing biological machine—I want what you love me with.

Even back when I thought Stoppard was merely clever, I might have seen that his was not only a theater of ideas. In 1975, as a young hitchhiker in England, I bought for ninety pence an upper circle ticket to the original production of *Travesties* at the Aldwych, with the great John Wood as Henry Carr, John Hurt as Tristan Tzara, Tom Bell as James Joyce, and Frank Windsor as Lenin. Stoppard's inspiration, allowing very different artists like Tzara and Joyce to meet Vladimir Lenin, is by itself enough to make one smile. His critique of the Russian Revolution happens here with a good deal less of the grief one finds in the later plays. Instead, we have the comedy of eccentricity, art and revolution seen through the faulty eyes of an old man losing his memory. Act Two of the play begins with a long discourse called "Cecily's Lecture," in which an attractive young librarian offers a potted history of Marxism. The speech seldom "landed" with early audiences, so Stoppard trimmed it and eventually cut the whole thing. Stoppard tells a lovely story, which Lee repeats in the biography, about a successful production of the play in Paris:

> . . . he spoke to the director and told him he didn't have to do the whole of that speech. "*Mais pourquoi pas? C'est magnifique,*" the director said. . . . After the play opened, they spoke again. How did Cecily's speech go? Stoppard asked him. "*Formidable,*

superbe," the director replied. "I was thinking, God, this is the sort of audience I deserve. So I go to Paris to see it . . . and he was right. She did every word and you could have heard a pin drop. But she was stark naked."

Stoppard is no snob. He understands what it means to be funny and why fun has meaning, why human beings need it. He came of age when commercial and subsidized theater were learning to work together. His plays have usually made money, sometimes piles of it, and he has also done plenty of writing for such popular entertainers as Steven Spielberg. He understands that in some ways art is a compensation for life as well as an illumination of it. Henry Carr's memories of Switzerland in 1917 may be unreliable, but that does not prevent him from seeing through the folly of his friends. Again, character is everything. You might say this is the theme of Lee's biography: the *character* of Tom Stoppard, even while he climbs socially and works relentlessly at his art.

I HAVEN'T BEGUN to touch on the breadth and variety of Stoppard's work, from the acrobatic electrons of *Jumpers* (1972), to his return to a childhood home in *Indian Ink* (1995), his use of the London Symphony Orchestra in *Every Good Boy Deserves Favour* (1977), his classicism in *The Invention of Love* (1997), or his collaborations with other playwrights like Václav Havel, who became a close friend. One of the joys of Stoppard's life, as recounted by Hermione Lee, is his many and varied friendships: Mike Nichols, David Cornwell (John le Carré), Harold Pinter and Antonia Fraser, the Duchess of Devonshire, etc. The fact that he was very good friends with conservatives like Paul Johnson and Margaret Thatcher has sometimes been held against him, and Lee takes pains to clarify his political beliefs. His plays may perform experiments, but they are not revolutionary or avant-garde. In fact, he seems to mistrust revolutionaries of all types, with the possible exception of the global eruption we call Rock 'n' Roll—his play on that subject runs a gamut from Sappho to the Rolling Stones. Yet Stoppard's kind of conservatism does not prevent him from casting a cold eye on things as they are. He has for much of his life been actively involved, through organizations like PEN and Amnesty International, with the problem of censorship and the plight of oppressed artists, scientists, and journalists all over the world. In a critique of contemporary British society, Lee notes, "he offered a random list: 'Surveillance. Mis-selling pensions and insurance. Phone hacking. Celebrity culture. Premiership football. Dodgy dossier. Health and Safety. MPs expenses. Political correctness. Internet porn. Targets as in the NHS. Managers as in the BBC. Bankers' bonuses.'" Plenty to agree with there. Most writers' lives appear to be entirely sedentary. Stoppard's is not. He is an active participant, not only in the theater of his time, but in the larger community. He has tried to be a good man.

That "simple enormous grief" I mentioned earlier underlies all of this effort, this kindness and generosity. More than once he has quoted a favorite speech from a play by James Saunders, *Next Time I'll Sing to You* (1962):

> There lies beyond everything . . . a certain quality which we may call grief. It's always there below the surface, just behind the façade. Sometimes . . . you can see dimly the shape of it as you can see sometimes through the surface of an ornamental lake the outline of a carp. . . . It bides its time, this quality . . . you may pretend not to notice . . . the name of this quality is grief.

Hermione Lee writes of all this with such skill that it never becomes maudlin, never seems to pry more than necessary into the man's privacy, never tries to sell us a psychological bill of goods. Her book contributes to the best writing about world theater since World War II, a kind of Elizabethan Age in which a vital theater shows civilization to itself.

Now you see it, now you don't. The very word theater comes from vision or spectacle. We have these things in movies, of course, but to sit in some kind of theater, shoulder to shoulder with our fellow citizens, watching living bodies act, is its own justification. Live theater has suffered in a time of pandemic and the advent of online streaming services, but I hope its magic will be returned to us. Are we losing the audience that could get all of Stoppard's jokes? Perhaps, but I suspect his plays will not vanish when he does.

2021

Two Poet-Critics

CLIVE JAMES AND JOHN BURNSIDE

Those who can't see the world in just one street
Must see the world.

—CLIVE JAMES

A heresy, but soul becomes
conceivable, immersed in viscera,
and mind endures, in wisps of meat and bone . . ."

—JOHN BURNSIDE

HERE'S A THOUGHT: literary criticism ought to entertain as well as illuminate. That puts most critics out of business on two fronts. So much of our exegesis reads like the minutes of a country club meeting in which *we are all agreed* on the value of this and that, so little of it chases the vitality literature itself is devoted to. Readers easily offended ought to toughen up and face the world in all its bloodiness. No one has permission to do anything in this life, so you might as well see what you can see, say what you can say, and do so as beautifully as possible.

These ruminations arise from a reading of two extremely good poet-critics, one a displaced Australian, the other a Scot.

They could hardly be more different from each other in their tastes and the tenor of their prose, but neither commits the sin of being boring, and both keep life itself clearly in their vision of poetry and its purposes. We may remember T. S. Eliot saying that a poet's criticism exists to elucidate the poet's own taste and ambitions. Certainly this is true of both Clive James (who died November 24, 2019) and John Burnside (still very much with us). Neither of them wields career-making power; both are masters of appreciation, a quality not so highly valued in the academy. Burnside is a good storyteller, a reader for whom context is everything, James a delectable raconteur whose prose (and verse) delights in antithesis. Both have spent their writing lives immersed in multiple genres, eschewing specialization. They are, first and foremost, writers.

The death of Clive James still leaves me feeling the planet is much diminished. What a bright spark of life he was, and in more ways than I can count. He was one of a generation of acclaimed Australians, including Germaine Greer, Robert Hughes, Bruce Beresford, Barry Humphries, and (from a decade earlier) Peter Porter, many of whom had to leave home to make their way in the world. James had been early recognized as a bright young man in Australia, but in England he had to scramble on Grub Street as a journalist and TV personality. No cushy academic life for him. He mucked in with actors, musicians, novelists and other sinners, obliterating distinctions of high and low culture by sheer force of personality and intelligence. One of his most famous aphorisms—"A sense of humor is just common sense, dancing"—touches the spriteliness of his mind. You can Google conversations he recorded in his library with writers, filmmakers, and other artists and you will be edified as well as entertained. Listen to him and Peter Porter talking about classical music, or the way he and Bruce Beresford could appreciate actors and movie stars. No other poet-critic I can think of has expressed so many opinions and enthusiasms on such a variety of subjects, including sports. He was voracious, and yet he retains an Australian perspective, not modesty so much as serious irreverence, the capability of delight. James wrote about *Game of Thrones* with the same pleasure he lavished on Dante—and rightly so. He understood the importance of vulgarity to art—how art can die of decorum if allowed.

As a writer, James is best known for his *Unreliable Memoirs* (1980) and other works of autobiography, but he also produced four novels, many books on travel and criticism, and a slew of poetry. Near the end of his life he published a translation of Dante's *Divine Comedy* (2013). His output was prodigious, much of it at a very high level. He just couldn't be pegged. So much of his best poetry was late-arriving that it will take some time to fully judge it. At his best, he was a very good poet, deserving comparison to Les Murray and A. D. Hope in Australia, and to his avowed master, Philip Larkin, in England. I'm not saying he was as good as Larkin because I don't know James's poetry well enough to say anything yet. I'm saying that Larkin was the yardstick by which he measured his poems, the modern English poet he loved best. If you love Larkin and love Clive James, you will welcome *Somewhere Becoming Rain*, the last book published in James's lifetime. It's a short collection, fifteen brief pieces in prose and verse, sometimes defending Larkin against the slings and arrows of other critics, sometimes just relishing Larkin's "compressed resonance" in a style of animated precision and aphoristic bliss.

Larkin was like "bottled lightning," James writes. "Speaking for myself, in my recent role as a frail old man, Larkin's verbal dynamism still tears me to bits." This comes from one of the best articles in the book, a review of Larkin's *Letters Home*, published just last year. Reviewing books by and about Larkin over the decades, James has produced a record of near-Boswellian fascination, aware that "Too much light has been shed" on the poet's private faults, too little on the perfection of his poems. James gets the very thing that makes Larkin valuable as a poet, not just the voice that "made misery beautiful," but also the stuff of poetry itself:

> In three essential volumes, the balanced triad of Larkin's achievement, all the poems are poised vibrantly in the force field of tension between his profound personal hopelessness and the assured command of their carrying out. Perfectly designed, tightly integrated, making the feeling of falling apart fit together, they release, from their compressed but always strictly parsable syntax, sudden phrases of ravishing beauty, as the river in Dante's Paradise suggests by giving off sparks that light is what it is made of.

Larkin's best readers, James among them, understand that mere despair is not the final product of the poems, perhaps not even one so dark as the late "Aubade." Larkin's art is part of it—the "ravishing beauty" of his phrasing—but there is also a whiff of something I can only call religious in a non-canonical sense, an awareness of secret harmonies, some of them just past our hearing.

That's why James's title, taken from Larkin's "The Whitsun Weddings," surely among the most perfect poems anyone has produced in English, is so apt. Here is Larkin's final stanza, after we have followed his point of view on a train journey toward London, seeing at each station a Chaucerian vision of life in its ordinary transcendence:

> There we were aimed. And as we raced across
> >   Bright knots of rail
> Past standing Pullmans, walls of blackened moss
> Came close, and it was nearly done, this frail
> Travelling coincidence; and what it held
> Stood ready to be loosed with all the power
> That being changed can give. We slowed again,
> And as the tightened brakes took hold, there swelled

A sense of falling, like an arrow-shower
Sent out of sight, somewhere becoming rain.

It's typical of James to notice from Larkin's letters that the final image was inspired by a movie, Olivier's *Henry V*. And who but Larkin would call life a "frail / Travelling coincidence," or take note of "the power / That being changed can give"? The diction is absolutely ordinary, the insight utterly profound. The phrasing itself is precisely what James seeks to identify and praise. Readers who attack Larkin for his personal failings, which were real, do themselves a terrible injustice if they neglect his extraordinary poems.

If James is a great defender of Larkin, Larkin was not always kind to James. His letters sometimes betray a typical anti-Australian snobbery when he writes to friends like Kingsley Amis. Yet at least once he defended James against an apparent slight from the novelist Julian Barnes: "And I like Clive James, because he praises my one unsuccessful book. Don't underrate him! He's a formidable character." James might have felt the sting when he read Larkin's letters, and he includes several kinder ones (previously unpublished) in this new book. The "one unsuccessful book" mentioned above was probably Larkin's *All What Jazz* (1970), which James reads as a key to the poet's aesthetic. He relishes Larkin's prose almost as much as his verse, saying it "flatters [the reader] by giving him as much as he can take in at one time. The delight caused has to do with collusion. Writer and reader are in cahoots." I can say the same about James's writing, which is very much like watching films of the man himself in conversation—lightly erudite, funny, congenial and inclusive. He assumes we can all keep up with him and never looks down his nose at life. "What the true artist says from instinct," he writes, "the true critic will hear by the same instinct." James was true to both art and criticism. Larkin is only one of his many subjects, but also a subject that could make his sentences sing.

IF LARKIN IS somewhere near the center of Clive James's poetic universe, he rates little mention in John Burnside's. In fact, Burnside sometimes seems to bear a Scot's grudge against certain forms of Englishness, preferring poetry from the Americas, north and south, and other points of the compass. Burnside's preferred Englishmen are figures like Lawrence and Auden, who left the country, or Sassoon for his objection to World War I. His book, *The Music of Time*, contains no mention of the likes of Ted Hughes or Geoffrey Hill. Clive James also had cosmopolitan taste. He notes, for example, unexpected similarities between Larkin and Italy's Eugenio Montale: "On music they often sound like the same man talking." It's worth remembering that James doesn't come to Larkin as a fellow Englishman, but as a colonial from the margins, one of an exciting generation of Aussies forging a new taste by their wits. He's not looking for political correctness so much as visceral eloquence. Larkin's taste in jazz is too conservative, but I see how it educated his ear, his phrasing. Clive James himself is nowhere near as parochial a reader or thinker. Nor is John Burnside.

The Music of Time is a large book, but a shapely and elegant one. It covers both familiar and unfamiliar poets, often placing them in biographical context or in fragments of memoir from Burnside's own life, and if his taste and mine sometimes diverge, I can still appreciate the fluency of his thinking and writing. Referring in a "Note to the Reader" to his twenty-three "vagabond and occasionally digressive chapters," he makes it clear that his book is less thesis-driven than associative:

> In short, my approach has been to step outside the more academic analyses of literature, and write about poetry responsively, which is to say, to discuss poems and ideas of poetry as they inform, not just "the life of the mind" but also my own day-to-day existence. For this is where poetry works best, in what Randall Jarrell calls "the dailiness of life"—and what

the poets discussed here have achieved, in the face of societal violence, rapid change, environmental degradation and the mechanization of almost everything, is a continuing, if sometimes minority, culture in which an appreciation of the everyday, and of the "irrational" (beauty, for example, or the sense of wonder) provides, not only a counter to overly mechanistic, procedural thinking, but also a basis for what might be described as a science of *belonging.*

His approach is learned, personal but not egoistic, narrative as well as delicately exegetical, always humane. He sees poetry—rightly, I think—as a way of resisting the many forms of violence imposed upon us by technological, commercial, and political powers. This is what Wallace Stevens meant by "the imagination pressing back against the pressure of reality," and it can take overtly public form, as it does in some poetry by Yeats, Auden, or Heaney, as well as in figures like Haki R. Madhubuti and Amiri Baraka, or in the sometimes foolish public actions of poets like Robert Frost, as well as in more private, quasi-religious gestures from the likes of Rilke. Burnside's book is never comprehensive, nor does it attempt to be. His good chapter on visual attention discusses Albrecht Dürer, Marianne Moore, and A. R. Ammons, but leaves out figures like Elizabeth Bishop and the very painterly Anthony Hecht. You will find broad coverage in this book, and you will be introduced to a few poets you've never read before—for me these included Albrecht Haushofer and Olga Orozco—but it's not a literary history or a survey course. It's a record of sensibility, an invitation to broaden one's thinking about the art and to make connections.

His chapter on race focuses on American poets, principally Black poets, so inevitably racism as it occurs in England or Europe or South America or China seems less in evidence, but that does not nullify the valid points he makes about the effect of violence on American poetry. He touches on violence as a sort of American ethos, including the violence of "cool" as appropriated by white culture:

> Back in 1963, when Steve McQueen, in a cutaway sweatshirt and specially tailored khakis, ran rings around a Nazi pursuit team during *The Great Escape*'s renowned motorcycle chase, the young, white, working-class Scots child that I was had no doubt that the word "cool" signified a form of anti-establishment self-reliance that was North American, almost certainly male, youthful (if not necessarily young) and most probably white, a mix of improbable charisma and elegant self-containment that only life's more fortunate sons could mimic.

It's an appropriate place to begin discussing the structures of American racism—by looking at the violence of masculine heroes, a brutality pointed inward as well as outward, as if all sensitivity has to be abraded and buried. From the impossible image of Steve McQueen, Burnside shifts to his own frustrations as a young factory worker: "I can still recall losing a good, fairly clean job when, aged nineteen, I 'hot-headedly' attacked a supervisor who was 'pushing me around'. . . ." The failure of cool, he writes, "can be disastrous in real terms, especially for someone who has dependents and debts." From here it's a short step to a failure of cool in Ralph Ellison's *Invisible Man*, and to the shootings of Black men by American police. Reading poets from Madhubuti to Gwendolyn Brooks, remembering as well the violence inflicted upon jazz musicians like Miles Davis, Burnside argues that the imaginative life is a way of keeping our most essential selves and souls alive. The dominant culture is, it might be argued, always criminal, and poetry is one of our hopeful subcultures—which is not to say it doesn't, like all forms of culture, develop class hierarchies of its own. Burnside's sympathy for underdogs, whether sinned against or sinning, seems integral to his person and his poetic.

Yet Burnside's appreciation of white American poets, by trying to sidestep one kind of hierarchy, falls victim to another.

The contemporary American poets he mentions are mostly those already approved by the creative writing industry, from William Matthews and Jorie Graham to Charles Wright and the late Lucie Brock-Broido, to whose memory the volume is dedicated. Having said this, in the face of his generous readings of world poetry and what he considers world culture, such carping feels petty. He can't possibly be comprehensive about American poetry, and he does write with generosity about canonical figures from Whitman and Dickinson to Frost. He is appalled by the racism in Stevens and Pound, but he also sees through Pound's madness to the grain of truth in his economic theories: "Whatever his flaws, Ezra Pound saw the dangers of runaway capitalism. . . ." And Burnside writes superbly about Hart Crane because he is sympathetic to unparaphrasable music, sound as being, which he usefully compares to the poetry of Dylan Thomas.

When he takes up the case of Robert Frost in a very good, central chapter, it's largely because Frost almost succeeded in making poetry relevant to the politically powerful—the very thing Yeats and Pound had also wanted. It's the romance of JFK, so seductive to our generation, the great lost opportunity America will never again be able to seize. Kennedy appeared to have a kind of panache lacking in figures like Nixon, and his respect for poetry and poets magically burnished the image of his presidency. Clinton and Obama have attempted to make this connection between poetry and politics as well, with mixed results. But wouldn't it be wonderful, if only . . . ? We can't really know. Was it JFK or was it his speechwriter, Theodore Sorensen, who produced the eloquence we poets admire? Well, we can add, at least Kennedy *sought* that eloquence. At least he saw what poetry might become in the public sphere. Burnside quotes the President's 1963 remarks during a memorial for Frost "at Amherst, just a month before his own death, a deeply moving speech in which he began by praising a poet who had once said, 'Were an epitaph to be my story I'd have a short one ready for my own. I would have written on my stone: I had a lover's quarrel with the world.'" Kennedy went on to say,

> Strength takes many forms, and the most obvious forms are not always the most significant. The men who create power make an indispensable contribution to the Nation's greatness, but the men who question power make a contribution just as indispensable, especially when that questioning is disinterested, for they determine whether we use power or power uses us. . . . The artist, however faithful to his personal vision of reality, becomes the last champion of the individual mind and sensibility against an intrusive society and officious state.

Burnside quotes more of this magnificent speech. I commend it to you as one of the high points in American political rhetoric. Would that it were all true.

Frost had already been compromised by his own ego. At the end of his life, ill and at times mentally confused, he made an ill-fated trip to Russia on Kennedy's behalf. He got along well with Khrushchev in their meeting, but bungled his report of it to the press, complicating international relations. Burnside tells the story very well, using honest reportage by the poet F. D. Reeve, who was along on the journey. Frost had been compromised in another way at Kennedy's inauguration, when he tried to read the poem he had composed for the occasion, the forgettable "Dedication," but was prevented by the glare of winter sunlight off the snow and marble monuments. Instead he recited "The Gift Outright," a poem I have never been able to stomach due to its approval of manifest destiny. It might be argued that the only truly good thing about Frost's relationship to Kennedy was the way it inspired the President's speeches. We could do with a lot more of that good spirit now.

ONE CAN QUIBBLE MORE with Burnside's excellent book. His moving chapter about poetry and grief brings in Rilke and Maria Tsvetaeva, but makes no mention of Tennyson, for example. I might guess it's due to a vaguely suppressed anti-English feeling, yet the chapter takes its title and epigraph from Shakespeare, albeit the Scottish play: "Give sorrow words. The grief that does not speak / Whispers the o'erfraught heart and bids it break." Burnside numbers himself among those who "persist in the sentiment that, in spite of everything, we are more Pict or Celt than Christian or Brexiteer." Not accidentally, his penultimate chapter is devoted entirely to Seamus Heaney, another figure who wrestled with the social responsibility of the poet. The fact that Heaney resisted simplistic demands where such responsibility was concerned, that he remained true to his vocation as much as his politics, is entirely laudable. Burnside writes,

> Admittedly, one poem is only a drop in the moral ocean, but a lifetime's work, especially an *oeuvre* that has become as much a part of the cultural fabric as Heaney's, becomes something more like a wave. To anyone reading Heaney the risible contention that poetry is politically ineffective is like saying that raising a child or planting a tree is a waste of time. It means nothing, because it gets the timescale wrong, and it ignores the law of unexpected consequences.

Hopeful words. And it should be remarked that Burnside's final chapter, "The Poets in Ghana," gets its title not from the Singaporean, Botswanan, and Native American poets it discusses, but from the ironic phrasing of a poem by Frank O'Hara, so multiculturalism is seen as both desirable and problematic, like the phenomenon of translation and the inevitability of cultural appropriation. Burnside's idealism is decidedly circumspect, while his sympathies remain useful and attractive. In his chapter on Albrecht Haushofer he writes,

I remember being told, as a child, that if you shine your torch beam up into the night sky, the light travels on for ever, to the very edge of the universe. And so it was, I guessed, with sound. Everything—all the music of what happens—travels out from the surface of the earth into farthest space. I have never been entirely sure that this is true (wouldn't the sound waves decay, eventually?) but I would like to think it is.

On second thought, he might consider the frightful noises humanity makes that would equally be inclined upward and outward into space. At the very least, poetry remains, in the eyes of Clive James and John Burnside, an attempt at the antidote.

2020

The Searching Stories
of Helen Garner

I ONCE OVERHEARD a writer friend in Melbourne calling the Australian writer Helen Garner "overrated." What she meant, really, was "ubiquitous." A writer can be seen so frequently that she invites contempt. In Australia, Garner is everywhere, or nearly so—as highly regarded and controversial as anyone, perhaps best known for her literary journalism on high-profile court cases and the excerpts from her marvelous journals now appearing in volumes that read like penetrating novels. Garner's journals demonstrate how profoundly she has observed her private life, how deeply she has sought integrity in both life and writing, how humane and funny she can be about her own foibles. To me, she is a model among contemporary writers for her independence of mind, her devotion to precision in prose, her beautiful irreverence. Recent collections of her essays and short stories only confirm my impression that, far from being overrated, Garner is one of the most compelling writers alive.

She has been called a minimalist by herself and others, but Garner packs a lot into small spaces. "At first you simply transcribe," she writes of her technique. "Then you cut out the boring bits and try to make leaps and leave gaps. Then you start to trim and sharpen the dialogue. Soon you find you are enjoying yourself." On the evidence of *Stories*, her collected short fiction, minimalism does not mean the usual pinched, semi-cerebral stuff we associate with the term. Garner's stories may be brief, but they contain expansive moments and room for the mystery of human motives. Her characters, simultaneously awful and comic, are so closely observed that they resonate like poems. Her prose is wiry, stark, precise, but to find her equal for the tone of generous humanity one has to call up writers like Isaac Babel and Anton Chekhov. This is a small book that feels large with life.

Known for both novels and journalism—writing that melds the personal and public, particularly life in Melbourne and its suburbs—she has also written film scripts for Jane Campion and Gillian Armstrong. Her own first novel, *Monkey Grip*, was made into a film, and the photographic precision of her prose, the way she lets her images hint at psychological depths her characters barely comprehend, feels tautly cinematic. Indeed, many of her stories sequence images like "glassy Canadian lakes flawed by the wake of a single canoe," or a young girl reacting visually to being talked about by adults: "She saw her own foot, in its large, strapped blue shoe, swinging awkwardly near her aunt's hip."

Garner writes about lives in which awareness has been submerged by fear. "Postcards from Surfers" evokes a family with the line "Everything is spoken, nothing is said." What does get said is a marvelous Australian vernacular. Here a woman's retired parents notice a car for sale with a license plate from Western Australia—the far side of this island continent:

> "Look at that," says my mother. "A WA number-plate. Probably thrashed it across the Nullarbor and now they reckon they'll flog it."

"Pro'ly stolen," says my father. "See the sticker? ALL YOU VIRGINS, THANKS FOR NOTHING. You can see just what sort of a pin'ead he'd be. Brain the size of a pea.'"

It's an ordinary moment, but it conveys the folk poetry of Australian conversation, the geographical knowledge that goes with it, the judgment and enjoyment of words, the way an Australian can at any moment become Odysseus narrating his life with spellbinding brio.

In another story, "La Chance Existe," a gay narrator steps into a strangely intimate dance with his friend, a heterosexual woman. In "Little Helen's Sunday Afternoon," the slapstick of preadolescence—a girl with her foot stuck in a bucket—comes smack up against the reality of sex and the horror show of a doctor's medical photographs: "The children were horrible. Their heads were bloodied. Their hair had been torn out by the roots, their scalps were raw and crisscrossed with black railway lines." The world observed here is both violent and merciful. The stories surprise like spontaneous discoveries.

Tough and unsentimental as she is, Garner writes as a mother and lover. She understands mystery and the uncontrollable forces of life in our very nature. One of her most beautiful endings occurs in "Civilisation and Its Discontents," when a middle-aged mother sees a pregnant woman "lumbering towards me, a woman in the final stages of waiting, putting one heavy foot in front of the other," and what she feels is envy: "Oh, let me do it again! Give me another chance! Let me meet the mighty forces again and struggle with them! Let me be rocked again, let me lie helpless in that huge cradle of pain!"

The 2017 edition of *True Stories*, Garner's collected nonfiction, begins with another mother, Akon Guode, "a thirty-five-year-old South Sudanese refugee, a widow with seven children." In a trance of desperation, Guode has driven her car into a lake, drowning three of her children. Garner sets to work as a journalist, trying to find out "Why She Broke." The essay feels entirely up to date in its implications of gender, race, and the law. But Garner has never been doctrinaire about anything, nor is she the sort of journalist who needs to arrive at definitive answers to impossible questions. The essay ends by alluding to *Medea*, the great tragedy of Euripides about a regal witch who kills her children.

One of her best essays, "On Darkness," concerns her willingness to examine the sometimes-gruesome photographs in Sydney's Justice and Police Museum—"the purity of the recording eye" and "the holiness of a place where something rich and final has happened." Garner trains her gaze on the moral gravity of her own writing: "I see now that for some years already I had been trying to turn myself into the sort of person who could look steadily at such things, without flinching or turning away. . . . I longed to mimic in my own work the brutal simplicity of the police photographs."

Her searching stories—a word in her case interchangeable with "essays"—have sometimes offended others. "The Fate of *The First Stone*," about her controversial 1995 book concerning a case of sexual impropriety, is the rational response of a mature feminist writer to another kind of feminism that had become "a bullying orthodoxy." Garner remains stubbornly patient, probing, curious about everything. In one of her best essays about writing, "The Art of the Dumb Question," she tells an interview subject, "Listen. I am one of the least boreable people you are ever likely to meet."

"At the Morgue" is typical of Garner's curiosity. "I would be lying if I claimed to be able to give a blow-by-blow account of the first autopsy I witnessed. The shock of it made me forget the sequence. Time slid past me at breathless speed." She describes the process in enough detail that it could make you lose your breakfast, then her curiosity deepens: "There is nothing so utterly dead as a dead body. The spirit that once made it a person has fled." Garner interviews the people who perform these miracles of close examination and becomes interested in them as living human beings.

Her own life interests her as well, and several essays in this large volume are personal memoirs of childhood, marriage, and divorce. "Sunday at the Gun Show" becomes a meditation on the pathos of masculinity, while "A Scrapbook, An Album" works by a series of aphorisms and vignettes. "Why Does the Woman Get All the Pain?" details how she got sacked from a teaching job in 1972 by talking honestly about sex to a classroom of thirteen-year-olds. The dialogue here is frank and funny and refreshing—unfortunately too obscene to be quoted in an American newspaper. Yet even here she finds a kind of sacredness in genuine human connections.

Garner's literary essays on writers like Patrick White, Elizabeth Jolley, Germaine Greer, and Tim Winton, bring to mind another great Australian, Clive James. And in "While Not Writing a Book, Diary 1" she quotes the *New Yorker* critic Joan Acocella's words about Mikhail Baryshnikov: "If there is a point in classical art where aesthetics meets morals—where beauty, by appearing plain and natural, gives us hope that we, too, can be beautiful . . ." Garner then adds her own note of recognition: "I resolve to spend the rest of my life searching for that point." These two volumes are a record of that search and a marvelous introduction to the beautiful, brutal simplicity of Garner's storied life.

2021

Robert Stone
and American Wreckage

That is my subject, America and Americans.

—ROBERT STONE, *THE PARIS REVIEW*, WINTER 1985

He bolts down all events, all creeds, and beliefs, and
persuasions, all hard things visible and invisible, never
mind how knobby; as an ostrich of potent digestion
gobbles down bullets and gun flints.

—HERMAN MELVILLE, *MOBY DICK*

IN THE OPENING SCENE of Robert Stone's breakthrough second
novel, *Dog Soldiers* (1974), a journalist named John Converse
finds himself sharing a park bench with a widowed missionary, "an American lady of middling age" whose "waxen color-
ing was like an opium smoker's." The bench faces Saigon's Tu
Do Street, known for its bar girls, and the year is something
like 1971, when Stone himself briefly reported on the war. The
conversation of these two Americans, a writer who has experienced schizophrenic episodes and a Christian whose husband
was tortured and killed by guerillas, quietly reveals the terrors
of an unhinged civilization, one side detached from any coher-

ence and the other convinced that the Apocalypse has arrived and God will take care of the just. Converse, fevered and paranoid, responds to this missionary woman in cynical confusion, like a man with no core or center of being, and even fantasizes about sleeping with her, only to be told, "We don't need interesting things." But Converse does. He shifts from one "interesting thing" to another with only the faintest exercise of his own will. Later in the novel, caught in a spidery disaster only partly of his own making, he tells his father-in-law, "I've been waiting my whole life to fuck up like this."

Ah, the 1970s, a time of violence and dissolution rather like the present, without the hopeful elements of the Black Lives Matter movement. No wonder a believer in the End Times is such a potent metaphor, and no wonder the nation reached in 1980 for Ronald Reagan and "morning in America," when little was being done, structurally or otherwise, to make the country a better place for the majority of its citizens. For many Americans, morning has more often been mourning. No wonder we acquiesced when Clinton repealed the Glass-Steagall Act, a little shot of heroin to the markets. Stone's remarkable novel finds in the moment something deeper, a contradiction, a festering absence underlying the country's idealism, its myths of heroic individualism and insane obsession with winning at all costs. Stone, who died in 2015 at age 77, would have had no trouble at all foreseeing the societal damage of Donald Trump's America. Ken Kesey, a friend from his early countercultural years, called him "a professional paranoid." The writer Steve Chapple, in a 1984 profile for *Mother Jones*, called him "the Joseph Conrad of Imperial America, chronicling decline and fall with an intensity and realism unmatched by any contemporary novelist." Stone is often compared to Conrad and Graham Greene for the seriousness of his writing, his psychological penetration and expansive vision of American wreckage, which also leaves wreckage behind in countries around the globe. How could a nation of such idealism, such potential, and such accomplishment produce so much trouble, both inside and outside its own borders? Well, look at its people, Stone seems to say, who are really just humanity unleashed, exposed, and in many cases unaccommodated. We all end up a bit like Lear on the heath.

Stone loved Shakespeare and sometimes acted in professional stage productions. He had from his youth a prodigious memory for poetry, and his characters, even his villains, are given to quoting bits of Hopkins or Yeats or Emily Dickinson. Whether or not they are educated, they can talk (and talk and talk), roughing out their own philosophies and justifications. He loves the gab of Americans, relates details of their houses, their clothing, their booze and cigarettes. He observes the minutiae of his characters' lives as well as any contemporary novelist I know. In addition to Greene and Conrad, his influences surely include noir and pulp writers and the great masters of American seediness like James M. Cain and William Lindsay Gresham. *Dog Soldiers* is Vietnam noir and, with its feckless drug dealers on the run, also seems a precursor to Cormac McCarthy's *No Country for Old Men*, which became an even better film by the Coen brothers. *Dog Soldiers* was also filmed as *Who'll Stop the Rain?* (1978), directed by Karel Reisz and starring Nick Nolte, Tuesday Weld, Michael Moriarty, and a ferocious Anthony Zerbe. Stone's first novel, *Hall of Mirrors* (1966), was filmed as *WUSA* with Paul Newman, Joanne Woodward, and Anthony Perkins—I remember that messy 1970 film as being saturated with a despair typical of the times.

Stone was a reader of American fiction as well as American lives, and the novel that most obsessed him might well have been Melville's *Moby Dick*. In the *Mother Jones* profile he says, "Melville is America's prophet. The white whale to me means the nonwhite world. It means nature. Ahab is not just America, but western man, constantly pursuing, obsessively going after and seeing as evil what he cannot subdue. To put it in Marxist terms, if the heroic age of the bourgeoisie was pursuing whales, then the post-heroic age is pursuing smack." That in 1984. Think of the opioid crisis now, and it seems little has changed. Stone's nonfiction essay about Vietnam, "A Mistake Ten Thousand Miles Long," also turns to Melville:

> "Vengeance on a dumb brute seems blasphemous." So the Quaker Starbuck in *Moby Dick* sought to reason with Captain Ahab.
>
> "Talk not to me of blasphemy, man," Ahab replied; "I'd strike the sun if it insulted me." He wasn't doing it for an abstraction, like victory or for the oil. He was a moralist in an immoral world and he was going to fix it.
>
> It's not gratuitous that *Moby Dick* is the great American novel and Ahab, with his passion for control and his "can do" spirit, is an American hero. Ahab started out chasing the whale because it represented everything that was wrong with the world. By the end of his disastrous voyage, no one remembered where goodness resided, and the whale and the whalers went down together in a victory for no one at all.

Robert Stone was never the victim of either/or thinking. His opposition to the war did not blind him to atrocities committed on both sides, and in the *Mother Jones* piece he calls postwar Vietnam "a state of geriatric Stalinists." Rather, he sees the whole debacle for what it reveals about humanity, which is also revealed by the contradictions of American society, its dark idealism and unwillingness to face the truth. Stone went to Vietnam because he wanted to write about America. He never lost sight of that vision; he pursued it throughout his life in novels of increasing sophistication, complexity, and grace.

NOVELIST MADISON SMARTT BELL rightly believes the time has come for a reappraisal of Robert Stone. He has published a biography, *Child of Light*, which I have not yet read, and two new collections of Stone's work: a fiction volume gathering the novels *Dog Soldiers*, *A Flag for Sunrise*, and *Outerbridge Reach*, which has been given the dignified imprimatur of the Library of America, and a volume titled *The Eye You See With: Selected Nonfiction*. All three of these books came out in 2020. In a published excerpt from the biography, Bell writes, "A Robert Stone novel is an artistically closed system in which the social issues of a given period play out in an experimental form." I'm not sure what Bell means by "closed" here, since the novels I've read shoot out their ideas and implications broadly, but Stone certainly developed his own way of shaping narrative fiction. "You construct characters and set them going in their interior language," he told *The Paris Review*, "and what they find to talk about and what confronts them are, of course, things that concern you most." While Vietnam touches most if not all of his books (several of his characters are veterans), the novels do seem realistic depictions of particular decades. *Dog Soldiers* is a Vietnam book set mostly in the United States. *A Flag for Sunrise* (1981) is primarily set in a Central American nation, Tecan, closely resembling Nicaragua on the eve of the Sandinista revolution. And *Outerbridge Reach* (1992) deals with another class of Americans, some of them Reagan Republicans, in an era of financial criminality. Each book focuses on three or four main characters, switching from one point of view to another as the narratives move forward. The separate lives intersect at important junctures, but each has its fully-developed arc, and each makes compelling reading in its own way. If Stone is particularly good with middle-aged male characters, he gives devoted attention to his women as well. They all seem alive and real. None are excessively idealized, and even their heroism is fraught with irony. "Irony is my friend and brother," Stone said in *The Paris Review*. His novels bring irony to a lyric pitch.

Yet realism might not be the best term to describe a Stone novel. Again in the *Paris Review* he said, "Realism as a theory of literature is meaningless. I can start with it as a mode precisely because I don't believe in it. I *know* it's all a world of words— what else could it be? I had the curious luck to be raised by a schizophrenic, which gives one a tremendous advantage in understanding the relationship of language to reality. . . . My mother's world was pure magic."

It's the magic side of Stone's world, verging on religious vision without its underpinnings of belief, that gives his work its most powerful compulsion. He's damned good at the novel form, but his novels always express more than their realistic plots imply. He seems to have thought of the form symphonically, as a large musical structure, which is why many of his scenes unspool with a logic wholly beholden to his characters' improvisations.

Stone's mother was intelligent as well as troubled. It was she who gave him Kerouac's *On the Road*, a book he later disliked, but which at first set his literary compass. When she was institutionalized for her mental illness, he was taken in by a Catholic orphanage, where his interior life met a strong spiritual and intellectual tradition. He was a street kid, but a smart one, and even in the Navy, where he served for three years, he carried a book of poetry. Stone landed in adulthood right at the moment of the Vietnam war, the Civil Rights movement, and the anarchy of Kesey's Merry Pranksters—he is mentioned in Tom Wolfe's *The Electric Kool-Aid Acid Test*. He knew Kerouac and based the character of Ray Hicks in *Dog Soldiers* partly on Neal Cassady, as Kerouac did with Dean Moriarty. One can find such allusions throughout his work, always transmuted by the demands of the novel at hand.

Yet Stone himself was resilient. Having experimented with every drug on earth and battled his own alcoholism, he survived the era with his brain fully operational, his eyes open, his powers of observation capable of growth. He was a grown-up, an artist fully devoted to his craft, and throughout his work he exercised those powers of observation. In the Navy, he witnessed a French air attack on Port Said: "It was a slaughter of civilians. But it always is." In his later life he lived among prosperous people in Connecticut and Manhattan and Key West.

The milieu of *Outerbridge Reach* is not far removed from that of John Cheever—people with money who are always close to being people without money. If there's an aspect of genre fiction to some of Stone's work, it's always deepened and complicated. Reading *A Flag for Sunrise*, one feels the influence of Graham Greene, especially in the character of Sister Justin, a Catholic nun sympathetic to the revolutionaries. Then there is Pablo, a killer and druggie cut loose from his American life. The true protagonist or authorial stand-in, Holliwell, is an anthropology professor at the end of his rope. One of his old CIA pals from Vietnam days tries to recruit him to spy on the missionaries in Tecan and he refuses. But he also burns most bridges in his life and allows himself to be implicated in the danger. His motives include a sort of midlife crisis, distaste for the hypocrisies of conventional life, a worldly curiosity combined with unwitting innocence.* Tecan's police and revolutionaries are as thwarted and human as Conrad's anarchists in *The Secret Agent*. One of the revolutionaries says, "Small suffering countries don't require ironists. When we require ironists we'll produce our own. Without help from the United States." Another says, "*Compadre*, we are all vulgarizations of history. We have to live it out by the day— life, unlike sound philosophy, is vulgar." Stone's willingness to risk vulgarity in his storytelling gives it vitality and truth.

Even in his self-destruction, Holliwell demonstrates an attractive sensitivity that might in other circumstances have become religious. During a beautiful scene in which he goes diving on a reef, we are allowed to see his awareness of nature: "The icy, fragile beauty was beyond the competency of any

---

*Stone's introduction to a Penguin edition of Greene's *The Quiet American* is collected in the nonfiction under review here, a very smart piece of critical prose in which he says, "To be innocent is to be bumptious and stupid, rude, provincial, inconsiderate; well intentioned but at the same time conscienceless and murderous."

man's hand, even beyond man's imagining. Yet, it seemed to him its perfection provoked a recognition. The recognition of what, he wondered. A thing lost or forgotten." The scene is so good I can't resist quoting more of it:

> Some fifty feet away, he caught clear sight of a school of bonito racing toward the shallows over the reef. Wherever he looked, he saw what appeared to be a shower of blue-gray arrows. And then it was as if the ocean itself had begun to tremble. The angels and wrasse, the parrots and tangs which had been passing lazily around him suddenly hung in place, quivering like mobile sculpture. Turning full circle, he saw the same shudder pass over all the living things around him—a terror had struck the sea, a shadow, a silence within a silence. On the edge of vision, he saw a school of redfish whirl left, then right, sound, then reverse, a red and white catherine wheel against the deep blue. It was a sight as mesmerizing as the wheeling of starlings over a spring pasture.

We know this is not mere pretty nature writing because in the novel's opening scene something terrible was done on that reef. Young people are being murdered, their bodies dumped, and even the fine old missionary, Father Egan, is compromised by these doings. The fact that Stone never says explicitly what changes in that water, the shudder passing there, leaves it in the realm of religious mystery. It makes sense that Holliwell's path should cross with Sister Justin's—a man searching for faith in *something* and a woman who has given up theology for revolution.

Holliwell tells Sister Justin that she is being used by the revolutionaries, and she responds, "At last, thank God." Her torture and death are more obliquely written, making use of the Emily Dickinson lines from which Stone derives his title:

A Wife—at daybreak I shall be—
Sunrise—Hast thou a Flag for me?

At Midnight, I am but a Maid,
How short it takes to make a Bride—
Then—Midnight, I have passed from thee
Unto the East, and Victory—

The victory is, of course, sadly ironic, as is Holliwell's final confrontation with the killer Pablo, and the dark meditations on history arising from it. Stone's ability to make us feel both sympathy and revulsion at his characters demonstrates his maturity as an artist.

IF GENERIC CONVENTIONS of the crime novel and the political thriller animate *Dog Soldiers* and *A Flag for Sunrise*, something else—the sailor's yarn of Melville and Conrad—functions in *Outerbridge Reach*, the subtlest and most intriguing of the Stone novels I have read. Here the authorial presence is more diffused, split between two very different men. The first is Owen Browne, an Annapolis graduate and former Naval officer (service in Vietnam, of course), now earning a living selling yachts to the rich. Browne is a non-drinker (very rare in Stoneland), a Republican, a man who disapproves of cursing but also a man for whom the conventional life has never been the only solidity. His is an American life leaned on absence, an apprehension of the abyss held at bay by his family life, his work, and his friendships. When he reunites with old Navy pals, we see their valid and divergent lives, but also their disappointments:

Their lives were bound in irony, Browne thought. Not one of them had chosen the Navy on his own. Each had been impressed into the Academy by the weight of someone else's expectations. In the case of Ward, it had been family tradition. Browne and Teodor were the sons of ambitious immigrant parents. If they had all graduated from high school only a year or two later they might have resisted. He and his friends had been the last good children of their time.

Earlier we saw Browne soloing in a leaky sailboat, and we know from the novel's opening that all is not right with the world:

> That winter was the warmest in a hundred years. There were uneasy jokes about the ozone layer and the greenhouse effect. The ambiguity of the weather made time seem slack and the year spineless. The absent season was a distraction. People looked up from their lives.

There's a spare, visionary poetry in Stone's prose, which only gets richer and more complex as the book progresses. This is not a novel about global warming but about something at least as enduring and troubling: human character.

The second major character in the book, Ron Strickland, works as a filmmaker. His Vietnam documentary infuriates people like Browne, and in the book's opening we find him trying to complete another political film on a Central American revolution. Both men are lured into another project by corporate figures eager to save their business fortunes through a kind of distraction. A wealthy businessman and yachtsman, Matty Hylan, has gone on the lam to avoid criminal charges. Browne decides to take Hylan's place in a round-the-world yacht race, and Strickland accepts money to make a film about it. Their enterprises end in disasters revealing the characters of these men, and also the society in which they function. Both men, salesman and artist, want to believe in their own abilities but are riven by doubt. Both are filmmakers—Strickland an artist perhaps compromised by his distance from humanity, Browne the writer and star of corporate videos. In the end, we can see both men as artists of a sort, trying to make art out of life with its criminal compromises. The conventions of family and country have been the only coherence for Browne, yet he experiences moments of beauty and love within them. His wife, Anne, also becomes a major character in the book, a woman fighting her own disillusionment and compulsive behavior. All of them must make choices and must act, their actions driven by character, by need and desire.

Like Stone himself, Strickland has a stammer he sees as a weakness, and his childhood is a trouble he can't shake. Human weakness defines him as an artist:

> One day, he thought, he might make a film of the fairgrounds and its ghosts. He had never used old photographs and the music would be fun. No one would claim he was repeating himself. When his taxi pulled up in front of the Finnair terminal, he was deep in contemplation.
>
> Stepping up to first class check-in, he found himself reluctant to part with the fantasy of a different film. The ones unmade were always pure. But in his heart he knew that there would never be such a venture, that he would never celebrate old fairgrounds or migrating salmon, threatened rain forests or Ojibway pictographs, or any of the other worthy subjects that sometimes occupied his daydreams. Strickland was devoted to the human factor. It was people he required.

As with all artists, we are left to wonder when he's being ruthless and exploitative, when he's engaged in actual revelation. Stone must have felt implicated in the actions of all three of his major protagonists, which is why he knows them inside and out.

Browne the hero goes to sea on his voyage, but soon turns anti-heroic and duplicitous, lying to himself and others, making up his voyage as though he were dictating a novel by radiophone. We arrive at his crime, if that's what it is, through intensely beautiful passages of derangement. He has moved beyond social strictures, moral guidelines. He has become a sort of Kurtz figure immersed in the horror, though ultimately he tortures no one but his own family. Strickland claims to be after the truth in his films, while Browne finds a terrible truth in hallucination, or seeing through the scrim of reality:

At sunrise, when Browne went up on deck, there was a pale blue shimmer over the northeastern horizon. Staring at it, he saw something inexplicable.

In the center of the glow was what appeared to be an inverted mountain range. Peaks hung upside down like stalactites, their points barely touching the surface of the sea, thickening to a central mass a few degrees above the horizon. It was as though an upside-down island hung suspended there.

He stood for a long time staring at the strange sight. The inverted peaks were delicate and beautiful, flashing ice colors as the sky lightened. He turned the boat toward them. After about thirty minutes the sight vanished. But where the line of ice had been, a single petrel soared on the wind, ranging ahead of the boat at a constant bearing, as though it were leading him on. Impelled by some urgency like hope, Browne steered his vessel after the bird's passage.

The image is like something out of Swift or Coleridge. Stone sees that complete scandal, complete annihilation of any pretense of virtue, underlies much of our heroism. In the end, Browne's widow, Anne, seems to understand what he must have experienced, and decides to set out on a voyage of her own.

I have not begun to convey the closely-observed social detail of the novel, only its metaphorical rudiments, but the whole effect is profound. In that *Paris Review* interview I have found so illuminating, Stone says, "The purpose of fiction is to help us answer the question we must constantly be asking ourselves: Who do we think we are and what do we think we're doing?" Notice that Stone asks us what we *think*, not what we actually are. He would never presume to know.

2020

The Inner Exile
of Dana Gioia

1. The Outsider

> As Marx maintained and few economists have disputed,
> changes in a class's economic function eventually trans-
> form its values and behavior.
>
> —DANA GIOIA, *Can Poetry Matter?*

To understand Dana Gioia's contribution to modern American
poetry, one must first acknowledge his position as an outsider.
This will seem strange to some, who consider Gioia the ulti-
mate insider, a man with his fingers in many cultural pies, a
man of privilege, educated in the Ivy League, prosperous, pro-
lific, and political. Dana Gioia the corporate poet, who had
attained a vice-presidency at General Foods when he resigned
his position there to write full time. Dana Gioia the co-author
(with superb assistance from his wife, Mary) of popular text-
books used in many of the colleges and universities of the
United States. Dana Gioia the Bush appointee as Chairman
of the National Endowment for the Arts, the man who talked
a hostile Congress out of more money and in effect saved the
institution he ran for six years. An originator of programs

devoted to reading, Shakespeare, jazz, the writing of returning veterans, and Poetry Out-Loud, a marvelous program helping high school students develop skills in thoughtful performance. A man much honored in the public realm, his shoulders bowed by eleven honorary degrees—he could joke with Robert Frost about being educated by degrees, but unlike Frost he had already earned several the old fashioned way, as a student. Dana Gioia the co-founder of a prominent poetry conference held each June in West Chester, Pennsylvania. A manager of people, hiring and firing and running the show like some Republican Wizard of Oz. Until his retirement in 2020 we have had Dana Gioia, professor at the University of Southern California, able to make a living by teaching one semester a year without having to attend faculty meetings. Surely no one has ever been so privileged.

These external trappings, however, are not purely privilege but the result of Gioia's feisty independence and clarity of vision, a clarity deriving precisely from his status as an outsider. To be an insider is to lose privilege in its root sense, "a bill or law affecting an individual." To be an insider means to behave as part of a group, a tribe or social class, and this Gioia has never done. He has maintained his privileged status as a contrarian, a visionary, and he has made enemies in the process. "Give me a landscape full of obstacles," he says in a poem called "Rough Country," and you know he means obstacles in multiple ways. One of his favorite Shakespearean lines comes from Duke Senior in *As You Like It*: "Sweet are the uses of adversity." Gioia is not a Duke, but has had to claw his way up from working class roots, the son of a Mexican-American mother and a Sicilian-American father. He received a rigorous Catholic education that no doubt helped him succeed at Stanford University, where he took a BA and confirmed his desire to be a writer (he was also a serious musician and linguist). At Harvard he studied Comparative Literature, taking classes from both Robert Fitzgerald and Elizabeth Bishop along the way. Like other poets in a scholarly program, he was a double agent, unsure how to reconcile his creative ambitions with increasingly theoretical and arcane modes of study. He disliked what was happening to literature in the academy, and also saw how few options he would have for making a living if he continued on this course. So he did something outlandish. He went back to Stanford and got a Master's in Business Administration. As the dutiful oldest son in a large family without wealth, he knew he would have to make money.

I know I've used the word privilege perversely in some respects, reversing the usual expectations that come with it, but I want to differentiate real individuality from group thinking. Despite our protective tenure, we academics very often enforce the assumptions of our tribe concerning money, class, politics, literature, and theory. Often we write for each other, not for a presumed audience outside our walls and corridors. There is a strangely hidden pressure to fit in, to enter the fold, and the flock can behave cruelly toward an outsider. The corporate headquarters Dana Gioia entered also had its group behavior, its cruelties, but Gioia could put on its uniform, survive by its rules, hide his identity as a poet while he made a living, and look back on the academic world with the privilege of apartness. To do so, however, took prodigious, even obsessive and exhausting work—ten hour days at the office, plus late nights writing at home.

It was about this time—the late 70s and early 80s—when Dana and I began the correspondence that would lead to our friendship. We bonded partly as outsiders who loved aspects of poetry that seemed disallowed by the academy at that time— a sweeping generalization, I know, but we felt acutely that to love Robert Frost or W. H. Auden or Emily Dickinson or Richard Wilbur was to be thought insufficiently barbaric and American in the classrooms of the day, where poets who had been responding to the Vietnam war practiced their own violent righteousness, where race and gender politics were understandably coming to the fore after years of neglect. A generation of American poets born in the 20s and 30s had largely abandoned traditional techniques like narrative, rhyme, and meter to forge a poetry they considered more authentic, and we were simply young writers who still felt affection for diverse techniques and wished to keep them along with all the other tools at a poet's disposal.

I won't belabor what used to be called "The Poetry Wars" or waste time elucidating the cultural debates of the era. Others have done that *ad nauseam*. My purpose here is to understand Gioia's outsider status. It's not just that he made his living as a businessman, working late into the night several days a week on his poetry, essays, and reviews, keeping his literary life a secret from the steel and glass office—I actually visited General Foods with him in the early 80s, saw the security measures for entry, the sterile rooms, the glass ceiling beyond which unseen demigods maneuvered. Sacrificing a more romantic image of the artist, Gioia maintained his privileged outsider status, feeling no pressure to conform to academic criteria. He could write whatever he wanted, not what might have been required for tenure.

Though strongly associated with a poetry movement called New Formalism—and here I should acknowledge Wyatt Prunty's seminal study, *"Fallen from the Symboled World": Precedents for the New Formalism*, as well as books by many other writers—Gioia was steeped in the Modernist poetries of Europe and always wrote free verse as well as metered poetry. He maintained a devotion to narrative verse when it was utterly unfashionable in the university, and as a reviewer he proved small 'c' catholic in his tastes. He had a knack for seeing the talents of others and promoting them when no one else would do so. He had, in short, something in short supply in the literary world—integrity. And he was beginning to shape his independent vision in some of the most trenchant essays by any poet of his generation.

Dana Gioia is an outsider. He always has been. And the adversity he faced by writing outside the academy allowed him original insights, just as exile liberates Shakespeare's Duke:

Sweet are the uses of adversity,
Which like the toad, ugly and venemous,
Wears yet a precious jewel in his head;
And this our life exempt from public haunt,
Finds tongues in trees, books in the running brooks,
Sermons in stones, and good in everything.

But in his poetry Gioia's outsider status has more private meaning, dramatizing a profound schism between public and private identities. His increasing visibility in the public sphere has paradoxically moved him to guard private experience and make it the true subject of his poems. He has always written as a Catholic—large 'C'—in a secular age, has never allowed his subjects or forms to fit the expectations of others. And his major subject is that of the outsider, the inner exile, the man who cannot completely reconcile public and private realms, and who never feels that he belongs anywhere. He is a poet of psychic separation, longing for the intimate touch from which we have fallen, and it is from this intensely private grief that he has forged his humane and human vision.

2. The First Three Books of Poetry

Here feel we but the penalty of Adam . . .
—*As You Like It*, Act II, scene i

When I first visited Dana in New York in 1981—at last meeting the literary brother with whom I had corresponded for years— he kept me up half the night reading poems by someone I had never heard of. This was a poet of quiet lucidity, irony, and dramatic flair, a poet whose personae were death-obsessed and strangely thwarted Americans. The poet was Weldon Kees, whose reputation had evaporated after his apparent suicide in the 1950s. Donald Justice had with typical generosity edited a *Collected Poems*, and Dana would later edit Kees' fiction and drama. Poets desire fame, I suppose, but they adore obscurity, partly because it is so central to their own lives, their own fear of insignificance. The lives of people like Kees represent the dreams America fosters and destroys in equal measure. Kees would also influence Gioia's technique, most obviously in the verbal fugue, "Lives of the Great Composers," which made such an impression on Howard Moss that he imitated it in a poem dedicated to Dana. Gioia's "Lives of the Great Composers" is Keesian in its irony, observing how even artists who might tremble at the sublime come, like all chimney-sweepers, to dust. "Liszt wept to hear young Paganini play. / Haydn's wife used music to line pastry pans." The poem arises from Gioia's own vision of a fallen world where, as he says elsewhere, "Gravity" is "always greater than desire."

Those words are quoted from "The Burning Ladder," the poem opening *Daily Horoscope*, Gioia's remarkably assured first book, published in 1986. Though its poems vary greatly in form and subject, they are clearly the work of a refined sensibility—witty, knowing, haunted. Half a dozen of the poems are explicitly about the business world, a handful evoke the poet's native California. There are dramatic monologues and narratives as well as lyrics—something we find in all of Gioia's poetry collections. The verse is formal but never rigidly so, lucid and even plain in a manner we sometimes associate with other Stanford poets from Yvor Winters to Timothy Steele. Yet Gioia's technique feels less obviously like technique, and I imagine the influence of Elizabeth Bishop, as well as poets writing in other languages, might have contributed to this flexibility.

Whatever landscape Gioia writes about—New York, California, Italy—and whether his poems are set in airports or offices, bedrooms or the out-of-doors, he never evades the central problem of his work—this schism between public and private, dream and reality, the workaday world and the imaginal. "The Journey, The Arrival, and the Dream," a remarkable narrative from *Daily Horoscope*, is about a woman traveling through the Italian Alps. The journey itself seems nearly arbitrary, purposeless: "Journeys are the despair before discovery, / you hope, wondering if this one ends." Addressed in the second person as if by her own daimonic inner voice, the woman arrives at a hotel, but in the poem's dream logic nothing connects. She even writes "a letter in a language" she doesn't understand. The rarified beauty at which she has arrived, the sublime, is uninhabitable.

> Emptying your pockets on the dresser, notice
> how carefully you put down all the useless keys
> and currency you've brought from home, so terrified
> of scratching the patina of the varnished wood
> that innocently reflects the lamp, your hand, the curtains,
> and the badly painted cherubs on the ceiling
> who ignore you. Light a cigarette and watch
> the lazy smoke creep up and tickle them
> to no effect and realize you don't
> belong here in their world where everything
> is much too good for you, and though the angels
> will say nothing, they watch everything you do.

You don't belong. Those three words recur in Gioia's work—most conspicuously in his latest book, which I'll delay discussing till the end of my essay. Gioia's theme of unbelonging, the exiled self, can be understood biographically, of course, in the way a working-class kid might feel at Harvard or Stanford or, for that matter, in the White House. But while I do think those three words, *you don't belong*, are the psychic key to all of Gioia's work, I should also point out how he dramatizes them, turns them into something other than mere confessionalism.

Like Eliot, he transmutes the private into lines of broader psychological significance.

The lines I've just read are also Catholic. There's the displacing guilt of being watched by angels, the apartness from art's cherubic bliss. For Gioia, Catholicism has been a complex inheritance. On the one hand it is a house for the dispossessed, a home in which one is never fully at home. It's also a cultural tradition, connecting his Mexican and Italian roots to Rome, putting his languages in one basket, as it were. Here I pause to connect my beginning with my end. To understand Gioia's first book, I quote from one of his more recent publications, "The Catholic Writer Today":

> Catholic writers tend to see humanity struggling in a fallen world. They combine a longing for grace and redemption with a deep sense of human imperfection and sin. Evil exists, but the physical world is not evil. Nature is sacramental, shimmering with signs of sacred things. Indeed, all reality is mysteriously charged with the invisible presence of God. Catholics perceive suffering as redemptive, at least when borne in emulation of Christ's passion and death. Catholics also generally take the long view of things—looking back to the time of Christ and the Caesars while also gazing forward into eternity. (The Latinity of the pre-Vatican II Church sustained a meaningful continuity with the ancient Roman world, reaching even into working-class Los Angeles in the 1960s, where I was raised and educated.)

Even in poems that have nothing overtly to do with Catholic subject matter, Gioia depicts a fallen world and the suffering of the individual desiring grace, which might also be understood as a sort of unity of being.

One further point. Because Gioia is also a Westerner, a city boy who grew up with access to sublime and relatively unspoiled nature, the natural world remains a saving presence in itself. It is evidence of God. Terrence Malick, in his film *The Tree of Life*, explicitly pits the natural world and its animal laws against the grace of God. Gioia is a California Catholic who has read and understood the nature poems of Robinson Jeffers and others, has read praise of nature in poets like Gerard Manley Hopkins. His notion that "all reality is mysteriously charged with the invisible presence of God" makes him on the whole less eager to transcend the body, more willing to admit immersion in the world as a way of being.

And yet this grief, this unbelonging, this schism, this inner exile. Both forces are at work in Gioia. The sexual histories of his characters always have something secret and illicit about them. The first book contains "My Secret Life," a poem in which the words of a Victorian pornographer morph into another of those daimonic second-person narrators:

No other details of your life survive,
    and so your secret will be kept
forever. Now you are only what you wanted
    to be: a scholar of seduction,
certainly more the antiquarian than lover,
    and these pages catalogue a life's
accumulation of encounters with the same obsessiveness
    an eccentric would bestow
on a collection of exotic stamps: clipped,
    soaked, separated, and arranged
by year and origin neatly in an album
    until it is almost unbelievable
that every one could bring a human message.

That message might be love, but can a pornographer say it? The title poem of *Daily Horoscope* turns the second person into the hectoring voice of the astrologer, those newspaper columns in which we mirror meaning for our lives. Another lovely lyric, "Cuckoos," takes up the folklore in which the birds are emblems of betrayal, but points out that "the Chinese took their call / to mean *pu ju kuei, pu ju kuei*— / *Come home again, you must come home again.* . . ."

Where would that home be, and could he ever belong in it? The book's final poem, "Sunday Night in Santa Rosa," is set where Gioia would eventually come to live, in a house on a hill in northern California. But the poem is not restful. It's about a carnival packing itself up to hit the road again:

Off in a trailer by the parking lot
the radio predicts tomorrow's weather
while a clown stares in a dresser mirror,
takes out a box, and peels away his face.

Gioia's second book, *The Gods of Winter*, appeared in 1991. In the five years between these two books he had faced the greatest crisis of his private life—the death of his first-born son, Michael Jasper, of Sudden Infant Death Syndrome at only four months. As Dana had comforted me when my older brother died in 1979, I found myself trying to offer solace to a friend who was literally staring into the abyss. Many friends tried to comfort Dana and Mary. But there is no solace and there is no comfort in the face of a child's death. I mention this because it relates to my theme of exile. Gioia's position is no intellectual exercise. It is born of raw feeling and trauma and grief. This awareness of loss, even extinction, has made him the poet and critic he is, a patron of the unrecognized, the unseen, and a poet who knows all about the unsaid.

Two short poems in the second book stand at the poles of his life. The opening "Prayer" comes from the Catholic as well as the grieving father, addressing God in metaphors:

Seducer, healer, deity or thief,
I will see you soon enough—
in the shadow of the rainfall,

in the brief violet darkening a sunset—
but until then I pray watch over him
as a mountain guards its covert ore

and the harsh falcon its flightless young.

That harsh falcon could of course come from Jeffers or Hopkins, secular and Catholic at the same time.

Another short poem, "Money," is in freer verse, and in fact
adapted from the prose of his essay "Business and Poetry."
"Money" gets a laugh in performances and represents Gioia's
rueful take on pecuniary realities. But just like "Prayer" it is a
list poem, a series of metaphors or slang terms, using as its epigraph a metaphor from Wallace Stevens: "Money is a kind of
poetry." It's one of several Gioia poems in which the efficacy
of language itself is challenged. Poetry and prayer inhabit a
realm apart from the man of action who effects change in the
world. Gioia had by now a reputation as a businessman poet,
often compared to Stevens, or to figures like James Dickey or
A. R. Ammons. People in my own profession, teaching, look
down their noses at the business world, and Gioia bore a lot
of criticism for his chosen life. But I also know the choices he
had made were becoming worrisome to him. The privilege of
independence he had earned with no small measure of courage
allowed him to be the writer he wanted to be, but it was also
killing him and he knew it. His own mother could see it, too,
and would eventually advise him to quit business and strike
out on his own.

These personal details may cast some light on the struggles
of the poems, the effort to reconcile public and private realms
made more difficult by the elder son's responsible nature. Two
long narrative poems in *The Gods of Winter*, dramatic monologues in the voices of very different personae, emerge ironically from that nature. "Counting the Children" is in the voice
of an accountant, Mr. Choi, who must tally the estate of a

deceased old woman, a collector of dolls. Choi is the responsible man of business, but also a kind of artist: "And though you won't believe that an accountant / can have a vision, I will tell you mine." His vision is of childhood, of individual nature. The weird non-lives of the dolls he has had to count have given him nightmares; he feels their contempt for our fragile humanity—again like that traveler under the ceiling's cherubs, the transcendent mocking the ordinary. The second monologue chills in another way. "The Homecoming" is in the voice of a mass murderer driven to hatred by the love of the woman who raised him. Her moral righteousness served only to underline his essential illegitimacy.

> But as I stood there gloating, gradually
> the darkness and the walls closed in again.
> Sensing the power melting from my arms,
> I realized the energy I felt
> was just adrenaline—the phoney high
> that violence unleashes in your blood.
> I saw her body lying on the floor
> and knew that we would always be together.
> All I could do was wait for the police.
> I had come home, and there was no escape.

The desire for arrival has a dark side. The idealism of a killer overcomes the idealism of a world that would correct his nature.

The Gods of Winter contains some of Gioia's most soulful lyrics about grief, including the title poem and "Planting a Sequoia." It also contains "Rough Country," which I cited in my opening, and his gorgeous poem about belonging, or nearly belonging, "Becoming a Redwood":

> Stand in a field long enough, and the sounds
> start up again. The crickets, the invisible
> toad who claims that change is possible,

and all the other life too small to name.
First one, then another, until innumerable
they merge into the single voice of a summer hill.

Like his first collection, both varied and accomplished, offering poems in rhyme and meter as well as free and blank verse,
The Gods of Winter confirmed Gioia's reputation, as they say,
yet was relatively ignored in establishment circles, where he
was dismissed unjustly as a formalist conservative, the devil
who had dared to criticize the creative writing programs.*

Gioia's third book, *Interrogations at Noon*, won the American
Book Award, signaling that he might not be ignorable as a poet
much longer. Coming a decade after his second book, the new
collection also demonstrated the toll his busy life exacted on
his creativity—it simply took him longer to finish enough good
poems to make a collection because, having left business in
1992, he was so busy working as a freelance writer and editor.
The book contains more translations, song lyrics, and oper-
atic arias than earlier collections, and though these first-rate
pieces are by no means padding, a careful reader will wonder
why there are fewer new poems on offer—the one big dramatic
monologue is from his superb translation of Seneca's *The Madness of Hercules*. "The world does not need words," says Gioia's
opening, and the poet in this volume is certainly more austere
and self-critical. The dry noon of mid-life interrogation makes
the book feel chastened, as if trying to suss out where to go
next. Among the masterpieces of the book I would single out
his blank verse lyric, "Metamorphosis," the only poem I have
space to give you in its entirety:

There were a few, the old ones promised us,
Who could escape. A few who once, when trapped

The Gods of Winter, it should be said, fared very well in England as a
"Choice" of the Poetry Book Society, which in turn gave Gioia opportunities to work for the BBC and cemented several friendships abroad.

At the extremes of violence, reached out
Beyond the rapist's hand or sudden blade.

Their fingers branched and blossomed. Or they leapt
Unthinking from the heavy earth to fly
With voices—ever softer—that became
The admonitions of the nightingale.
They proved, like cornered Daphne twisting free,
There were a few whom even the great gods
Could not destroy.

              And you, my gentle ghost,
Did you break free before the cold hand clutched?
Did you escape into the lucid air
Or burrow secretly among the dark
Expectant roots, to rise again with them
As the unknown companion of our spring?

I'll never know, my changeling, where you've gone,
And so I'll praise you—flower, bird, and tree—
My nightingale awake among the thorns,
My laurel tree that marks a god's defeat,
My blossom bending on the water's edge,
Forever lost within your inward gaze.

The language here is simply beautiful, and that's where I want
to leave, momentarily, my consideration of Gioia as a poet, and
turn to other things.

3. Criticism, Translations, and Libretti

> I was attracted to poetry long before I ever thought of
> writing it . . .
> —Dana Gioia, *Can Poetry Matter?*

Of course, Dana Gioia is more famous as a critic and public
servant than as a poet, but I wanted to set aside that fame—or

infamy as some would have it—to consider the work of most importance to him. Now that I have begun to do so—there's still one more book of poems to go—I'd like to look briefly at the larger picture. The private grief of the poet is one thing, the public utterance of the critic quite another, but both are possible because of Gioia's outsider stance, his privilege of apartness.

The first criticism I saw from Dana came in his book reviews for Stanford literary magazines, then for *The Hudson Review*. These reviews astonished me, educating me about poets I had never heard of. He taught me how to read poets as different as Radcliffe Squires, Jared Carter, and Ted Kooser, reminded me of German and Italian poets and obscure Californians, regional poets and poets with eccentric lives. As a West Coast boy whose upbringing was more prosperous but also more provincial than Gioia's, I needed instruction badly, and it was Dana's criticism more than anyone else's that gave it to me. He's not a close reader like Helen Vendler—she lodges that complaint against him in her *Paris Review* interview. Gioia's criticism works outside accepted academic modes in two very different ways. On the one hand, we have his essays of sociological diagnosis, standing at a distance from the literary world and examining it in the context of a culture the academy often fails to see, let alone acknowledge—the culture of people who are not poets and professors. On the other hand, we have appreciations of neglected masters. Here Gioia is not only the protector of the uncanonical but a teacher of remedial reading. Do you think anti-populist modernism has swept the field? Gioia responds with a lengthy defense of Longfellow. Are you sure the long poem is a measure of magnitude? Gioia tells you about Samuel Menashe, the great bohemian master of mind-expanding miniatures. Among the California writers he has reminded us to read are such utterly different figures as Kenneth Rexroth, Jack Spicer, and Kay Ryan. Critics who labeled Gioia a conservative have neglected to notice how broad-minded his tastes really are. No other writer of our time has devoted so much energy, so many felled trees and pots of ink, to resurrecting poets the academy assumed were safely dead or just invisible.

Try an experiment. Look at the tables of contents of every book of criticism devoted to modern or contemporary poetry, and you will see something curious. The same poets get discussed over and over again, as if we really needed another essay on Bishop or Lowell or Ashbery or Graham. Now look at Gioia's collections of critical prose and you will see how far outside the kingdom he has walked, and how clearly he has seen the fields around the castle. When Gioia does write about a canonical poet—Robert Frost or T. S. Eliot, for example—it is because he has something fresh to say about the work or the life. Gioia's essays are among the very few that make us better and broader readers. He leaves the close reading to us, trusts our intelligence, and simply reminds us to take a look at figures we might have missed in our busy lives.

His most controversial essay remains "Can Poetry Matter?", which caused much consternation on its appearance in the *Atlantic Monthly*. For one thing, people in my profession—and I do teach creative writing as well as literature courses—felt assaulted. They *were*, of course, but criticism needn't be felt so personally, and the attack was delivered with such reasonable civility that it hardly constituted terrorism. Gioia never said there was no such thing as a useful creative writing class—after all, he had studied with Miss Bishop at Harvard, which was a lot more creative writing than I ever got. Instead he pointed out an obvious truth: that people in a particular job begin to act as a group, sharing particular assumptions, protecting their own and each other's interests. This is simply true. I see it whenever I look in at MFA programs or wonder about new anthologies. The cronyism is still there, still self-protective, still more about keeping the job and publishing than promoting great poetry.

In fact, while it is statistically true that poetry "matters" a great deal in America right now, with more money and publicity to back it up than ever before, it is equally true that the contents of most magazines and books of poetry are spectacularly dull. I am one reader who finds far more poetry in a good novel than in most contemporary poems. This is more than a grouse. It is a crisis for the art, and the smug response of many poets to Gioia's criticism does them no honor. I have met writers with MFA degrees who do not know the history of their art and do not understand the rudiments of traditional techniques like meter. Their education in self-worth has, frankly, been a sham. They have paid poets to tell them they are wonderful, which is not the most valuable lesson for an artist to learn.

"Can Poetry Matter?" was the title essay of Gioia's first critical collection, published in 1992. The book had something to infuriate everyone: an essay on "Business and Poetry" reminding us that there was more than one way to make a living, a skillful attack on "The Successful Career of Robert Bly," a piece called "Notes on the New Formalism," which was a non-polemical look at forgotten techniques, and essays on regional poets unknown to the arbiters of taste. One of them, Ted Kooser, has since been Poet Laureate and won the Pulitzer Prize, a fate also befalling still another of Gioia's "discoveries," Kay Ryan. When Gioia was asked to judge a first book contest in 1999, he chose an unknown young poet from Georgia named A. E. Stallings.

Each of Gioia's essay collections, including *Disappearing Ink: Poetry at the End of Print Culture* (2004) and *The Barrier of a Common Language: Essays on Contemporary British Poetry* (2003), contains work that is prophetic, taking the long view, and useful in what it teaches about reading. Gioia the critic translates, or carries over poetry from its academic ghetto to the common reader. He anticipated the connections between poetry and such popular phenomena as rap before they were taken up in the universities. In short, it is impossible for me to convey how much good he has done for the arts in America, and it surprises me how slowly and grudgingly some American artists will admit it.

Gioia's devotion to the modernists as well as the classics shows in his work as a translator from Italian, German, Latin, and other languages. He is simply one of the best verse translators we have at work today. And he translates in other ways, too, in his work with composers and musicians. His original opera libretti, including *Nosferatu* and *Tony Caruso's Final Broadcast*, are masterpieces of modern verse drama. No contemporary poet has taken a deeper interest in the genre of the art song, or has done more to promote the work of contemporary classical and jazz composers.

My discussion of these activities leaves much out, of course, but it also explains why we had to wait more than a decade for a new collection of poems. In his six years running the NEA, Gioia surely wondered whether he would ever write poetry again. But the muse did not desert him. Poetry came back, haltingly at first, and the new book proves that, while he may feel exhausted by his battles, he can still write like an angel.

4. *The Inner Exile and the World*

> Now you are twenty-one.
> Finally, it makes sense
> that you have moved away
> into your own afterlife.
>
> —Dana Gioia, "Majority"

Gioia is the sort of poet who would rescue populism from the charge of stupidity. He has always been a reader of the popular, including science fiction and ghost stories, and his poems frequently touch on the supernatural, being set in graveyards, or offering prayers, or otherwise keeping that Catholic eye on the afterlife. In some ways the most remarkable poem in his book, *Pity the Beautiful* (2012), is the long dramatic narrative at its center, "Haunted." A classic ghost story, its source is the psychic schism I mentioned earlier, both a class division and an inner one, a divided soul. A young man is in love with a rich, spoiled, and callous young woman named Mara. They visit her family's sumptuous home in the Berkshires and have the place to themselves for their dining and lovemaking—the Massachusetts setting also suggests they could be students at Harvard, or otherwise denizens of economic privilege. The speaker is clearly an outsider, appreciative of all that money buys, hopeful for his love life, but uncertain how to behave among such glamour. After a spat with his girlfriend, he wanders off alone in the cold, palatial house, which is very much a gothic movie set. In the library he reads Shakespeare's sonnets: "What is your substance, whereof are you made, / That millions of strange shadows on you tend?" And then, of course, he discovers he is not alone. Another woman is there. A ghost.

> We stood there face to face, inches apart.
> Her pale skin shined like a window catching sunlight,
> both bright and clear, but chilling to the touch.
> She stared at me with undisguised contempt,
> and then she whispered, almost in a hiss,
> "You don't belong here. No, you don't belong here."
> She slowly reached to touch me, and I ran
> leaving behind both Shakespeare and my shoes.

The language here is simple and clear, serving the story more than luxuriating in the rich textures of sound we might get from a poet like Anthony Hecht. But you can see this is the ghost that has haunted Gioia all his life—the voice that sees him and knows he does not belong, the judging voice that drives him and finds him wanting. The poem even whips up the sort of surprise ending we might find in popular fiction, and there again it stands outside the sort of writing usually found in contemporary poetry magazines. Thankfully, *The Hudson Review* has always saved a place for narrative verse, and that is where "Haunted" first appeared.

Now in his sixties, Gioia has not escaped these hauntings, these real and imagined presences, but *Pity the Beautiful* contains poems suggesting he may be ready to let them go. To be sure, some works in this collection are very dark, even chilling, like the masterful "Special Treatments Ward," one of the best things he has written in years. "So this is where the children come to die, / hidden on the hospital's highest floor." I can hardly bear to read the rest of this painfully honest poem.

Still, Gioia does mean *joy*. He's a man with much to be thankful for, including his wife, Mary, and his two living sons. His "Prayer at Winter Solstice" is a praise poem, and "Majority," the beautiful lyric closing the book, finds new meaning in Michael Jasper's early death—how death resembles other ways of maturing and moving on. The book's title poem has been compared by Bruce Bawer to Frost's "Provide, Provide," and it may be that a more resilient stance has arrived in Gioia's poetry. After all, he has his Catholic continuity, his belonging among the exiles. And one hopes he is done with public service, ready at last to let others take the heat and to acknowledge his own gifts. In his essay on Catholic writers he maintained that "Nature is sacramental, shimmering with signs of sacred things." It may be something else, of course—just nature, a meaning of its own. But how astonishing it is, this world we are given to see, however briefly and however much it hurts us. We don't need to feel belonging in order to see the blessings where they are, the shimmering gifts, the world's beautiful otherness, tongues in the trees, books in the running brooks, and sermons in stones. Among these gifts I would number the works of Dana Gioia.

2015

"The Song Is Drowned"

MICHAEL DONAGHY

LATELY I'VE BEEN telling people that the best poet of my generation is dead. No doubt it's ludicrous of me to nominate anyone as "the best poet of my generation," a phrase born of eulogistic hyperbole, however true it may feel. Yet when I re-read Michael Donaghy, a poet I knew and who was my senior only by a few months, and when I think of his death at age fifty in 2004, I flounder in the magnitude of the loss. Of course, the loss to his wife, Maddy Paxman, and their son, Ruairi, beggars what the rest of us may experience, but I would still like that amorphous entity known as "the poetry world" to acknowledge Michael's talent and accomplishment. And I hope more readers will discover the pleasures and depths of his work. He was a poet of bountiful erudition, energy, and delight. Even his haunted moods, his premonitions of an early death, came on with the brightness and wit of an Ariel.

Michael's *Collected Poems* and a collection entitled *The Shape of the Dance: Essays, Interviews and Digressions* appeared in England after his death, but failed to get much notice in the United States. A misguided review of these two books in the

TLS (August 14, 2009), treats Donaghy as a second-rate Paul Muldoon, and puts me perhaps too much on the defensive. Anyone who heard him perform—always from memory—will never forget his spontaneous gestures, the way his recitations felt like inventions. His best poems and prose pieces remain as performances even without his voice tipping them so precisely into our hearts. He was a clown in the best sense of the word, an irreverent, mercurial magician. He would have laughed at anyone who thought such qualities beneath the dignity of a poet.

Donaghy held three passports—Irish, British, and American—yet in the US where he did most of his growing up he is still too little known, while in England he was celebrated widely. British papers covered his passing with a breadth and thoroughness no living American poet would receive in his homeland; that and the posthumous publication of these two indispensable books demonstrate something of his impact. Yet I can't help feeling more needs to be said. Donaghy was one of the contemporary masters of dramatic voice in verse, and this is true of his lyrics as well as his sequences and dramatic monologues. His best poems succeed not just on the level of subject, line, and stanza, but as dramatic contrivances, entered into and shaped with ecstatic precision. If readers occasionally feel bored by the leaden sincerity of American poetry, they could do with a dose of Donaghy.

The modern era has given us plenty of mid-Atlantic writers whose nationality is sometimes difficult to pin down, from Henry James to T. S. Eliot, W. H. Auden, and Sylvia Plath. Donaghy was an American whose language found an angularity and freshness in part from his appropriation of British and Irish idiom. His urban settings, particularly New York, Chicago, and London, seem engulfed by his personality—or perhaps I should say his personality was enlivened by their environs. He was born in the South Bronx in New York, a rough neighborhood that left him with memories of "horrific street violence" and racial tension. His parents were Irish immigrants who worked at a hotel in Manhattan—his mother as a maid and his father in the boiler room. When he was still quite young they made a stab at repatriation to Ireland, but gave up when work failed to materialize. Back in New York, they found jobs again, played Irish music, and conveyed an autodidactic appreciation for the arts. A favorite story about Michael happened in his teens when he worked as a doorman on Park Avenue—material he would use in his poem "Local 32B": "The rich are different. Where we have doorknobs, / they have doormen—like me, a cigar store Indian / on the Upper East Side, in polyester, in August." Already a poetry aficionado, he kept a volume of Hopkins hidden under his uniform cap. When none of his employers was looking, he removed the hat, opened the book and read. One day he was caught in the act and promptly rewarded for his transgression. The wealthy woman who discovered his taste for poetry bought him a season pass to the reading series at the 92nd Street Y, where he got his first look at some famous writers.

Michael had the spirit of a busker, but we shouldn't romanticize his life as a performer so much that we forget his education. His undergraduate diploma came from Fordham University in New York, and he went from there to a prestigious PhD program at the University of Chicago—stopping short of that degree because the language and politics of the theory-ridden academy gave him the willies. Nevertheless, it remains clear from Michael's writing that some intellectual rigor—part Jesuit and part academic—stuck to him in spite of his rebellion. He knew what the fashionable theories were about, and his mind was supple enough to appreciate multiple types of poetry. He even edited poetry for *The Chicago Review*, which no doubt gave him a very good look at American literary politics. Yet, until he took on creative writing work in London in the last decade of his life, Donaghy made his living as a traditional Irish musician. Performing was in his blood, and the attendant drugs and alcohol were in his blood as well. He was something of a wild man until fatherhood compelled him to settle down.

When Donaghy arrived in London in the 1980s he had published a single chapbook of poems, but he was quickly taken seriously on the British side of the Big Pond. One of his roles was that of "village explainer," interpreting American poetry trends to baffled Brits. He became a prime exemplar of that "mid-Atlantic voice" I mentioned—other such poets include Anne Stevenson and Thom Gunn. But Michael may have seemed something new—traditional and postmodern all at once, charming and riotously funny, turning sedate literary attitudes on their heads. He must have seemed a challenge to established writers even as he inspired younger ones. In America he was virtually unknown until the West Chester University Poetry Conference introduced him to an enthralled audience. To this day, his work has yet to find a major American publisher or significant critical champion.

Shibboleth, his first full-length collection, was published by Oxford in 1988 and won the Whitbread Prize as well as the Geoffrey Faber Memorial Prize. Donaghy would later admit that the book was over-praised in comparison to *Errata* (1993), his second. Some poems in *Shibboleth* do strike me as shallow exercises, but others remain among his most memorable. The management of conceit in "Machines," for example, comparing bicycle riding to harpsichord playing, echoes the Metaphysical Poets. (The *TLS* critic objected that Purcell didn't write harpsichord pavanes, but in fact he did write at least two pavanes, one of which Michael could have heard performed on a harpsichord.) Or the saucy defiance of "Pentecost":

> See? It's something that we've always known:
> Though we command the language of desire,
> The voice of ecstasy is not our own.
> We long to lose ourselves amid the choir

Of salmon twilight and the mackerel sky,
The very air we take into our lungs,
And the rhododendron's cry.

And when you lick the sweat along my thigh,
Dearest, we renew the gift of tongues.

That leap into apparent nonsense with "the rhododendron's cry" may irritate some readers, but it arises from the intimate glossolalia of sex. Makes perfect sense to me.

The title poem, "Shibboleth," with its mix of collusion and alienation as soldiers try to suss out spies, attracted readers looking for a postmodern stance—playful, skeptical of resonance:

One didn't know the name of Tarzan's monkey.
Another couldn't strip the cellophane
From a G.I.'s pack of cigarettes.
By such minutiae were the infiltrators detected.

By the second week of battle
We'd become obsessed with trivia.
At a sentry point, at midnight, in the rain,
An ignorance of baseball could be lethal.

The morning of the first snowfall I was shaving,
Staring into a mirror nailed to a tree,
Intoning the Christian names of the Andrews Sisters.
"Maxine, Laverne, Patty."

Readers of early Auden and Ashbery would be at home with this, as would theorists fond of discussing "language communities." Even as he writes of "Intoning the Christian names," Donaghy is irreverent. In the same book we find him inventing a medieval Welsh poet, Sion ap Brydydd (d. 1360) and offering seven of his poems. He loved hoaxes and poking fun at the pretense of critics, who, as he implies in his one major essay, are like wallflowers at a party.

For me, the two best poems in *Shibboleth* are "Remembering Steps to Dances Learned Last Night," a devastating dramatic monologue, and "The Tuning," which touches on self-destruction with a Keatsian beauty. In the former, Donaghy echoes Homer, Pound, and Cavafy, who in "Dareios" also wrote about the politically compromised career of the poet. Donaghy's speaker is fascinated by Odysseus, but in the king's absence he can't help befriending and entertaining the suitors. Most ironically, he is not even present for the central drama of his life:

> I know you came to hear me sing about the night the king
>   came home,
> When hero slaughtered hero in the rushlit hall,
> Blood speckling the white clay walls wine dark.
> I can't. I'd stepped outside when the music stopped mid-tune.
> Alone in the dark grove, I heard no sound but distant insects,
> And the sound of water, mine, against the palace wall.
> And then I heard their screams, the men and women I'd spent
>   that summer with.

He's like the dodging clown played by Bob Dylan in Sam Peckinpah's film, *Pat Garrett and Billy the Kid*, the sprite who appears so incongruous in a realm of fatalistic gunplay. I don't think Donaghy was in the least bit nihilistic, but neither did he make special claims for poetry's usefulness. His poets were jesters, not orators.

"The Tuning" opens grippingly: "If anyone asks you how I died, say this: / The angel of death came in the form of a moth / And landed on the lute I was repairing." As the speaker follows this angel "up through the thorn forest," she resembles the tiny Pooka in Flann O'Brien's *At-Swim-Two-Birds* somehow bred with the *aisling* of Irish poetry.

> That's when she started singing.
> It's written that the voice of the god of Israel

Was the voice of many waters.
But this was the sound of trees growing,
The noise of a pond thrown into a stone.

Donaghy breaks through the tissue of reason here, touching the uncanny. There's a rare sensitivity in the poem, a sense that life is just too painful to be lived:

I found a rock that had the kind of heft
We weigh the world against
And brought it down fast against my forehead
Again, again, until blood drenched my chest
And I was safe and real forever.

I teach this poem among others because I want my students to see real daring in writing, but I have to remind them that, whatever suffering he endured or brought upon himself, Michael was not a suicide. This extremity of feeling so fearlessly rendered comes from a man who wanted to live, whatever the ravages of booze and drugs.

Having said this, I should add that early in his second book, *Errata*, he placed a poem from the lower depths, "Acts of Contrition":

There's you, behind the red curtain,
waiting to absolve me in the dark.
Here's me, third in the queue outside
the same deep green velvet curtain.
I'm working on my confessional tone.

Here's me opening my wrists
before breakfast, Christmas day,
and here's you asking if it hurt.
Here's where I choose between *mea culpa*
and *Why the hell should I tell you?*

Me again, in the incident room this time,
spitting my bloody teeth into your palm.
I could be anyone you want me to be.
I might come round to your point of view.

With its violence and provisional sense of identity, the poem
seems more than a joke about Confessional Poetry. It's a night-
mare cut to sonnet length.

As I remarked earlier, Donaghy's distinction lies in his mas-
tery of dramatic voice. One source of inspiration in his work
was a fraught awareness of other people as well as a tenuous
sense of self. As a technician he worked not only by refreshing
traditional meters and free verse with an improvisatory flair
but also with a storyteller's instinct for the extraordinary. His
strongest poems are never static but are measured from scenes
in motion.

The centerpiece of *Errata* is a sequence of poems, "O'Ryan's
Belt," about musicians and the life of the itinerant player. Here
Donaghy celebrates a tradition akin to the blues—the learning
that takes place outside of books, freighted with its own lore of
obscure heroes:

I saw this happen. Or heard it told so well
I've staged the whole drunk memory:
What does it matter now? It's ancient history.
Who can name them? Where lie their bones and armour?

The erudition is musical as well as literary, governed by a
strong awareness of the ephemeral nature of our lives. The
tone of many poems is comic melancholia. Errata, after all,
are wanderings, strayings, even sins. The slips, mistakes, and
lost directions of a life govern much of the book—including a
fragmentary sequence on the Franklin expedition. Two final
poems about his mother involve stories, songs, and misappre-
hensions, falls from grace. Though I wouldn't want to claim

visionary status for his poetry, he was not without vision—partly that of a lapsed Catholic and a musician trying to get in tune. Someone better equipped than I will take up Michael's metaphysics. For me it's all mood, often sad, though never succumbing to the maudlin.

Like *Errata*, his third collection, *Conjure* (2000), is utterly assured in its manner. Critics have usually singled out the long dramatic monologue, "Black Ice and Rain," as a crowning achievement, but I agree with another reader, Jack Foley, that the poem is too close to Browning, too studied in its stance. Instead I prefer more playful work, like "Caliban's Books," with its wacky opening:

Hair oil, boiled sweets, chalk dust, squid's ink . . .
Bear with me. I'm trying to conjure my father,
age fourteen, as Caliban—picked by Mr Quinn
for the role he was born to play because
"I was the handsomest boy at school"
he'll say, straight-faced, at fifty.
This isn't easy. I've only half the spell,
and I won't be born for twenty years.

Or the film noir atmosphere (crossed with the Coen Brothers) of his drug-running poem, "The Drop," or the pure comedy of "Local 32B." Others have singled out "The River in Spate" as a strong (if unrhymed) sonnet. *Penetrar el espejo*, the dark refrain of his poem "The Years," again carries that anxiety about identity that animates his poetry from the start. And "Haunts" earns its title by addressing the poet's son from a spooky vantage point:

Don't be afraid, old son, it's only me,
though not as I've appeared before,
on the battlements of your signature,
or margin of a book you can't throw out,

or darkened shop front where your face
first shocks itself into a mask of mine,
but here, alive, one Christmas long ago
when you were three, upstairs, asleep,
and haunting *me* because I conjured you
the way that child you were would cry out
waking in the dark, and when you spoke
in no child's voice but out of radio silence,
the hall clock ticking like a radar blip,
a bottle breaking faintly streets away,
you said, as I say now, *Don't be afraid.*

The *Collected Poems* also contains the poems from *Safest*, a posthumous volume, and eighteen previously uncollected poems. I particularly admire "Southwesternmost" and "Two Spells for Sleeping" from *Safest*, and "Kaleidoscope" from the final section. A small poem called "Sharks Asleep" gives me the mournful title of this essay. Whatever his flaws and however incomplete his oeuvre may be, I believe Michael Donaghy's *Collected Poems* to be one of the most significant landmarks in contemporary poetry.

The importance of his criticism is not in its completeness—he left only one certifiably great essay and a few very good ones—but in the level-headedness he brought to aesthetic debates. Many of the pieces collected in *The Shape of the Dance* are brief reviews, answers to questionnaires, and other ephemera. They are all lively in their way, especially hilariously confessional pieces like "All Poets Are Mad." No fewer than five interviews with the poet appear in the back of the book. These tend to repeat material about his life, but contain useful indicators of his sources. By far the best prose from the middle of the book is his lecture called "American Revolutions"—a fine survey of trends in American poetry, useful in part because it tries to explain our squabbles to a British audience. Among other things, he puts to rest the myth that the fifties was a decade of academic stuffiness exploded by the Beats and the New York School. Donaghy informs us that several poets who

> are recorded as poets of the fifties . . . published their best work in the seventies.
>
> 1970 Elizabeth Bishop's *Complete Poems*
> 1972 James Merrill's *Braving the Elements*
> 1976 Bishop's *Geography III*
>   Merrill's *Divine Comedies*
>   Wilbur's *The Mind Reader*
> 1977 Anthony Hecht's *Millions of Strange Shadows*
>
> In my opinion, the last four books mentioned contain some of the century's greatest poems.

Donaghy's tastes were, in other words, *formal*, and he mistrusted self-aggrandizement of the sort often found among the Beats. For American poets of our generation, though, these elders were insufficient as models because they felt removed in their cocoons of literary success. That is why, for some of us, the slightly younger Irish masters, especially Heaney and Derek Mahon, became so important. They seemed unaffected inheritors of vital traditions, not slavish about form the way some of the New Formalists appeared to be. In fact, one of Michael's best observations about American poetry in the nineties was the rhetorical similarity of two divergent camps— the New Formalists and the Language Poets. Both claimed outsider status and both emphasized a break from a confessional poetic "middle ground" fostered in the creative writing programs. Donaghy understood the Language Poets and their fascination with critical theory without really wanting to be one of them. He felt more attunement with the avowed populism of the New Formalists, but found their proselytizing unpalatable. His own use of meter was more flexible and varied than some New Formalist poets allowed. When he reviewed *Rebel Angels,* a book I co-edited with Mark Jarman, he took full advantage of his international distance:

> Looking for convoluted tribal hierarchies, kinship rituals, and creation myths? Why parachute into some unhygienic rainforest when the culture of American poetry is an anthropologist's Disneyland? Here, segregated into traditions of the Raw, under the totem of Whitman, and the Cooked, under Dickinson, almost every poet declares an allegiance to his or her tribal "movement."

His review admitted some sympathy for the book because he knew how thoroughly such pleasures as meter and rhyme had been rejected by large numbers of American poets. British poets were unable to comprehend why Americans who used such techniques would feel embattled, but Michael patiently explained, over and over again, that such feelings had a basis in reality.

His great essay, "Wallflowers," subtitled "A lecture on poetry with misplaced notes and additional heckling," approaches aesthetics from the standpoint of the performer, pitting "The Shape of the Dance" against the blurry conceptualizations of the critic. "The terrifying truth is that form *substitutes* for logic. This is the poet's unique power, to address the passions in their own language, the very power that got us barred from the Republic." I can hear some of my academic colleagues tut-tutting that no art exists without the critic. True and not true. The critic cannot say everything the poem can *do*, as only a performer of poems would really know.

For Donaghy, prescribed forms were like a "pediscript," a drawing of dance steps—or rather, the patterns left by shoes in a dance floor's dust. "A player in such a tradition is expected to improvise, to 'make it new,' and the possibilities for expression within the prescribed forms are infinite." I would make his essay required reading in the academies of writing because it respects the mind but also represents the nature of artistic expression, the anarchic spirit freed when technique is mastered. Auden called poetry "a game of knowledge," and Donaghy would have approved of this definition. His essay begins,

> All my life I have harboured a weakness for those willfully eccentric philosophical and theological precepts valuable for their beauty alone, like Swedenborg's fancy that, in their purity and selflessness, angels create space instead of taking it up, thereby dilating the pin on which they dance, or the North African Gnostic idea that all material beings are 3D letters in the penmanship of God, or the Cabalistic fear that when, in the next great age, the Hebrew letter *shin* grows a fourth vertical stroke, a new sound will utter from men's mouths, making pronounceable the hitherto unpronounceable name of God—at which precise moment the world will end.

These affections, he admits, disqualify him "from the role of earnest philosopher," but he maintains the right to discourse upon his subject, which is "the relationship of the poet and the reader."

I'm not sure his essay presents any new information for students of aesthetics—he quotes figures like R. G. Collingwood, Frederick Turner, and Ernst Pöppel, alludes to Coleridge, Joyce, Borges, Bishop, and "the magus of unsupported assertion, Ezra Pound." What makes "Wallflowers" so beguiling is less its matter than its manner, the essay as comedic collage. But one idea undergirding the whole piece ought to be seriously considered by anyone who teaches:

> Imagine growing up in a society where one's first and only experience of music occurred in a schoolroom, where the beauty of music was meticulously analysed and explained to you and where you were judged by your ability to explain it in turn. In one sense your appreciation of music would be exqui-

sitely sophisticated because tunes wouldn't be tinkling persistently out of lift speakers or commuters' headphones. Music wouldn't be an "on" switch away, so you'd be more alert to its nuances when you did hear it. But let's face it, you wouldn't be queuing round the corner for the experience. It would always be more "improving" than pleasurable.

Of course, most of us don't come to music for the first time in school—we've heard it and made it for years before that. It's poetry, not music, which has become an art of classroom indoctrination, especially in the last century. As a first-rate performer, Michael knew that talking *about* the art could sometimes kill it, that the art was sometimes the very stuff that eluded criticism. I don't mean to appear anti-intellectual or to imply that Michael was anything of the sort. He was simply eager to be accurate about what we do when we say or dance a poem vs. what we do when we study it. At some point, theoretical approaches pale in the presence of actual performance.

Saying so will never satisfy "the earnest philosopher" or a certain kind of critic, nor does it seem you're getting your money's worth when a reader like me gushes about a lovely turn of phrase. Read him yourselves. Michael Donaghy will bear re-reading like few other poets of my generation. He conjures with a spiritedness that is far too rare among us. Bits of his work can be shrugged off, no doubt, but the best of it emits radiant creative energy. British readers have been lucky enough to have his books for many years, and now it is the rest of the reading public who should learn from what he left.

2010

Acknowledgments

Quotations in these essays not already in the public domain are often fragmentary or otherwise fall into "fair use" provisions of copyright law. Where more extended quotations occur, permission has been obtained as follows:

Sarah Bakewell, *How to Live: Or a Life of Montaigne in One Question and Twenty Attempts at an Answer.* New York: Other Press, 2011. Used by permission of the author.

Andrew S. Curran, *Diderot and the Art of Thinking Freely.* New York: Other Press, 2019. Used by permission of the author.

Michael Donaghy, *Collected Poems.* London: Picador, 2005. Used by permission of the publisher.

Dana Gioia, *Can Poetry Matter? Essays on Poetry and American Culture.* St. Paul, Graywolf Press, 1992. Used by permission of the author.

Dana Gioia, *Daily Horoscope.* St. Paul: Graywolf Press, 1986. Used by permission of the author.

Dana Gioia, *99 Poems: New and Selected.* Minneapolis: Graywolf Press, 2016. Used by permission of the author.

Dana Gioia, *The Catholic Writer Today*. Milwaukee: Wiseblood Books, 2014. Used by permission of the author.

Ovid, *Metamorphoses*, Charles Martin, trans. New York: W. W. Norton, 2004. Used by permission of the translator.

Alastair Reid, "Translator to Poet," from *Barefoot: The Collected Poems* by Alastair Reid (Cambridge, UK: Galileo Publishers, 2018). Edited by Tom Pow. Copyright @ 2018 by The Estate of Alastair Reid; @ 2019 by Leslie Clark. By permission of the Colchie Agency in New York. All rights reserved.

Kay Ryan, *Erratic Facts*. New York: Grove Press, 2015. Used by permission of the author.

photo by Cally Conan-Davies

David Mason grew up in Bellingham, Washington, and has lived in many parts of the world, including Greece and Colorado, where he served as poet laureate for four years. He is the author of eight books of poetry including *The Country I Remember, Sea Salt, Davey McGravy* (Paul Dry Books, 2015), *The Sound,* and *Ludlow,* which won the Colorado Book Award and was featured on the PBS *NewsHour.* He has also written a memoir and four collections of essays including *Voices, Places* (Paul Dry Books, 2018). His poetry, prose, and translations have appeared in such periodicals as *The New Yorker, Harper's, The Nation, The New Republic, The New York Times, The Wall Street Journal, The Times Literary Supplement, Poetry,* and *The Hudson Review.* Mason currently lives with his wife Chrissy (poet Cally Conan-Davies) on the Australian island of Tasmania, near the Southern Ocean.

CPSIA information can be obtained
at www.ICGtesting.com
Printed in the USA
JSHW022259140323
38969JS00001B/1